GW00418124

MALTA, GOZO and COMINO

Windrush Island Guides
include

LANZAROTE
MADEIRA and PORTO SANTO
MENORCA
CORFU

THE AUTHOR   Currently a Senior Lecturer in Geography at King Alfred's College, Winchester, Brian Dicks is also an experienced travel writer and the author of twelve books and many articles. Much of his writing has been on islands, including those of Greece, the Canaries and the Isle of Wight. His interest in Malta has led to a number of research visits and many more relaxing, and equally rewarding holidays.

MALTA, GOZO and COMINO

Brian Dicks

THE WINDRUSH PRESS
GLOUCESTERSHIRE

Acknowledgements
The author acknowledges the invaluable assistance of the National
Tourism Organisation of Malta in both London and on the islands. My
thanks are also due to Lothar Wuttke for help at manuscript level and
for the preparation of the Index-Gazetteer. I am further indebted to
Stewart Robertson for his work and advice on the photographs. Finally,
sincere thanks to the Windrush Press and the encouragement given by
Victoria Huxley at all stages of this book's materialisation.

First published in Great Britain by
The Windrush Press,
Windrush House,
Main Street,
Adlestrop,
Moreton-in-Marsh,
Gloucestershire
1991

British Library Cataloguing in Publication Data
Dicks, Brian
  Malta, Gozo and Comino.
  1. Malta. Travel
  I. Title
  914.58504

  ISBN 0-900075-02-3

Typeset by DP Photosetting, Aylesbury, Bucks
Printed in Hong Kong by Paramount Printing Group Ltd

Cover illustrations: (front) The monumental entrance to the church of
St Mary's, Mosta.   (back) The citadel and cathedral, Victoria on Gozo.

CONTENTS

This book is dedicated to
Anglo-Maltese Friendship
– past, present and future

INTRODUCTION

The Emblem Islands

Of the hundreds of thousands of annual tourists to the Maltese Islands a large proportion are return visitors. This is the best recommendation for any area of tourism and stands as proof that this small Mediterranean archipelago now provides the essential ingredients sought by increasingly discerning holidaymakers. Many return to enjoy the warm, sunny climate of these islands, their unpolluted seas, extensive provision for water sports, including modern yachting marinas, and varied night-time attractions. Others re-visit for different, but equally pleasurable reasons, not least to explore further Malta's fascinating countryside with its interesting flora, land use patterns and geological formations, the latter most spectacularly presented as exhilarating coastlines and seascapes. Then there are those, intrigued by Malta's eventful past, who return with the prime objective of indulging in its rich assemblage of prehistoric and historic monuments. Crammed within the small geographical area of these islands are early cave dwellings and Stone Age temple complexes, Roman villas and catacombs, medieval palaces, massive and richly ornamented Baroque churches, and some of the world's most impressive examples of military architecture.

Malta has been accurately described as living history and its monuments provide a detailed record of the many people who have been attracted to its shores. These have included ancient (and nameless) migrants, Greeks, Phoenicians and Carthaginians, Romans, Byzantines, Arabs, Normans, Spanish, the Knights of St John, Ottoman Turks, French and British. This remarkable pageant of cultures can be explained by the strategic location of the islands at the geographical centre of the Mediterranean basin. Consisting of the larger Malta, its sister island Gozo, the diminutive Comino and a number of rocky, uninhabited islets, the archipelago's combined area (see page 45) is less than that of the UK's Isle of Wight. Yet size is no reflection of past and present importance, for sentinel position in the narrows between Sicily and the North African coast has always governed Malta's identity and destiny. Not without just reason the islands have been called 'the Navel of the Inland

Position of the Maltese Islands

Sea', acting as colonising stepping-stones in times of peace and, more commonly, battlegrounds in times of conflict.

Historically nurtured by the frequent arrival and departure of migrants and traders, conquerors and rulers, the 'international' character of the Maltese is well-suited to dealing with the modern invasion of peoples – the vacationers and foreign 'second-home' residents. All are welcomed with genuine pride, friendship and understanding, though it has to be said that the rapid rise in property prices, a concomitant of foreign demand, has become a contentious local issue. Many non-Maltese residents are from the UK and British nationals still make up the largest group of tourists. A proportion of them are ex-servicemen and their families who were once stationed on Malta and return for a nostalgic look at how the islands have fared since independence. For them and other Britons, Malta is a 'home away from home', easy to accept and adjust to and, initially, to understand.

The universality of the English language is a major aid to the enjoyment of these islands by the British and other nationals and, whether they be black-attired grannies on Gozo or jean-clad youth in Sliema, visitors will find most islanders to be fluent English speakers. The Maltese are also proficient in other languages, especially Italian, but it is the British who sense the strongest feelings of *déjà vu* for there are other tell-tale remnants of what was once a persuasively ruling culture. For example, the Maltese have retained both the red pillar and wall-fixed post boxes which still display the royal insignia of the British kings and queens who, until recently, ruled the islands. Differently painted, though readily recognisable, are many old British telephone kiosks and it is not so long ago that the 'press button A or B' mechanisms were still operational. In Valletta and Sliema the St Michael and BHS stores carry a familiar range of goods, as do the local pharmacies advertising Boots'

The small church of St Cataldus close to Parish Square, Rabat

medicines and cosmetics. In the corner shops and mini-markets few British visitors will be denied the basic brand items they are accustomed to purchase at home.

But such things, especially today, are superficial trappings and observant visitors will quickly discover that Malta and its people are first and foremost the products of a proud native heritage and strong sense of national identity. Both firmly rest on the unique language of the islanders, which emanates from the east (see page 82), and their passionate Roman Catholic beliefs which they see as a fundamental link with the European world. Such cultural dichotomy is recognisable in other ways, not least in Malta's traditional domestic architecture whose style, still slavishly followed, blends both western and Middle Eastern influences. Geographically and historically the islands have acted as a Mediterranean assimilator and synthesiser of ideas and values, and through these age-long processes they have acquired their distinctive landscape and human characters. The locally acceptable level and speed of changes have always been measured against the precepts of religion and other deeply-held beliefs and these sustained the concept of a Maltese nationhood long before this was finally achieved in 1964.

Also called the 'Emblem Islands', the proudest of Malta's insignia is the country's flag which flies on all public buildings and adorns many others during national and religious holidays. It evokes much of the history and spirit of the islands for the white hoist and red fly are said to be the colours of Count Roger (see page 71) who freed Malta from the Arabs and returned it to the firm clutches of Christendom. In the top hoist corner is a much later addition, a representation of the George Cross awarded to the islands some 850 years later (see page 78) when, more than ever, strategic position continued to rule their fate.

Equally familiar is the Maltese Cross emblem which dates from the time when these fortress islands became the headquarters of the famous Knights of St John (see page 72). This distinctive eight-pointed cross is seen everywhere as the symbol of Air Malta and of the National Tourist Organisation of Malta. It is also the trademark of other firms and institutions, not least those still associated with the traditional ideals of the knightly order.

When the islands declared themselves a republic in 1974, another emblem appeared. Carrying the words 'Repubblica Ta' Malta', it was a pictorial representation of what was seen as the essence of this island state. Dominated by a large sun, whose powerful rays beamed across both sea and land, it highlighted Malta's traditional and on-going occupations.

In the sea section a decorated Maltese boat symbolised the continuing importance of maritime trade and industries and, resting on the land, the spade and winnowing fork paid tribute to the hard and dedicated work of the local farmers. Significantly, the large prickly-pear cactus, close to the sun's rays, emphasised the fact that the cultivation of these hot and dry lands has never been an easy process.

Known as the 'Symbol of Malta', recent governments have intentionally played down such traditional island images and, instead, have promoted the view of Malta as a Mediterranean growth point for further foreign trade and investment. It cannot be denied that Malta's feet are firmly planted in the present and the islanders are working for, and anticipating, an even more prosperous future. But much of this is reliant on the continuing expansion of the tourism market and, as mentioned, an increasingly large number of visitors are attracted for reasons other than the weather, water sports and night-life. In keeping with most popular tourism venues the Maltese Islands are faced with the conflicting economic and landscape pressures of further development and the need for conservation.

The following pages contain essential information for the first-time visitor's enjoyment of Malta. In addition, the detail on landscape, flora and fauna, history, economy and culture provide further bases for an appreciation of this fascinating country and its people. The islands are complex places which must be known to be understood and understood to be fully enjoyed. It is hoped that, like the author, its readers will become regular return visitors.

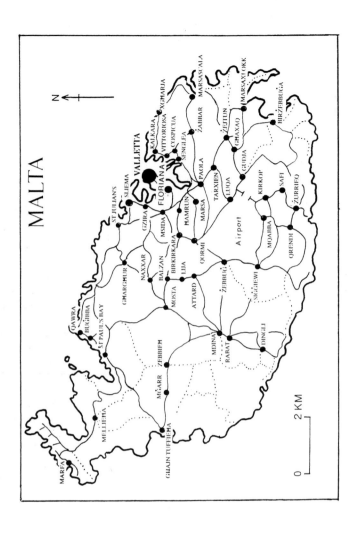

MALTA

GETTING THERE

By Air

The vast majority of Malta's annual visitors arrive by air on scheduled or chartered services. With British Airways no longer serving Malta, the national carrier, Air Malta, operates regular flights between Luqa Airport and London Heathrow and Gatwick, with other services to and from Manchester. Frequency and timings vary between summer and winter seasons. In addition the airline serves 15 other European cities as well as Cairo, Benghazi and Tripoli. The UK and Malta are also served by Monarch Airlines based at Luton, and Air Europe which uses Gatwick and Manchester. It should be noted that the latter airline is currently in financial difficulties and its immediate future is uncertain. A large number of charter flights (see page 9) also operate from most UK airports to Malta, the cost of all fares depending on the days and times of travel.

In the UK flight information for Air Malta is obtainable from Air Malta House, 314–316 Upper Richmond Road, Putney, London, SW15 6TU (tel: 081 785 3199), or from the Ticketing and Fares Office, 23–24 Pall Mall, London, SW1Y 5LP (tel: 071 839 5872-4). The airline's winter and summer timetable booklets contain a useful section on the principal seasonal events in Malta and Gozo. On going to print the address for Air Europe is The Galleria, Station Road, Crawley, West Sussex, RH01 1DY (tel: 0293 562626). Monarch Airlines can be contacted at Luton Airport, Luton, Bedfordshire, LU2 9NU (tel: 0582 422922).

In Malta offices of Air Malta are found at 288 Republic Street, Valletta; 28 Tower Road, Sliema; and First Floor, Luqa Airport. Numerous telephone numbers are quoted and visitors are advised to consult the local telephone directory. Air Europe is at 133 Manwell Dimech Street, Sliema (tel: 623455) and the representative of Monarch Airlines is Voyagair Ltd, National Road, Blata l-Bajda (tel: 234000 or 227372).

LUQA AIRPORT

The islands are served by Luqa Airport located some six

kilometres south of Valletta. It has suffered a lot of criticism by both passengers and airline companies, not least Air Malta itself which operates a heavy weekly flight schedule to and from the UK airports as well as to other destinations. Added to this is the use of the terminal by foreign airlines and with the massive volume of charter flights congestion is frequent and delays common. A recent letter to *The Times* (of Malta) questioned 'why it is necessary to go through hell to reach Paradise?' In fairness this old military airbase has undergone considerable enlargements and modernisation as former visitors who remember its notorious ramshackle appearance will vouch for. It also needs saying that many of the aircraft delays, hence the terminal's overcrowding, are caused by air traffic conditions beyond Malta's control. In summer, especially, this leads to a number of flights arriving and departing at roughly the same time. Conscious of the problem the Maltese government is fully committed to the policy of improving the efficiency of Luqa to meet Malta's annually increasing passenger needs.

Currently, ticketing and baggage handling facilities are inadequate and though boasting an air-conditioned restaurant and snackbars, these are frequently unable to cope with passenger demand. Shortage of space also means a small duty-free shop, but this particular problem is somewhat eased by the pre-ordering and payment for goods by departing passengers. Couriers and many hotels and tourist offices have the details. Another innovation is the availability of a duty-free shop to international passengers on arrival. Rather than carrying those awkward sealed plastic bags into Malta from the UK or other airports goods can be purchased prior to customs control – a useful distraction to the often tense period of awaiting baggage arrival. Luqa's duty-free prices are lower than those of many European airports.

The airport is poorly served by public transport though taxis are readily available (see page 16). Most visitors on package-holidays are taken to their island destinations and some hotels run an airport minibus for the independent traveller.

By Sea

The majority of passengers reaching Malta by sea will do so via Sicily, having initially crossed the Strait of Messina, the six kilometre-wide channel separating Sicily from southern Italy's Calabrian coast. This is an adventurous route, most visitors having used the rail services or autostrada that link Italy with the rest of Europe. This is also the main route for

The Strand waterfront along Marsamxett Harbour, Sliema

Maltese returning with cars and other bulky goods acquired from either visits or work periods in mainland Europe.

The Italian line, Tirrenia, operates regular services between Malta and the Sicilian ports of Siracusa and Catania, and on to Reggio de Calabria. In addition, there are less frequent crossings to Naples. The agents for Tirrenia in the UK are Serena Holidays/Maltavillas, 40–42 Kenway Road, London, SW5 0RA (tel: 071 244 8422). The company's main agent in Malta is S. Mifsud & Sons Ltd, 311 Republic Street, Valletta (tel: 232211). The Sea Malta Company Ltd, Flagstone Wharf, Marsa (tel: 232230 or 232239) operates a weekly passenger and car ferry service to and from Marseilles and Livorno, and the Gozo Channel Company, as well as operating the Malta–Gozo ferries (see page 17), provides regular services for passengers and vehicles between Malta and Catania. This crossing takes about eight hours though for passengers only Virtu Rapid Ferries (3 Princess Elizabeth Terrace, Ta' Xbiex, Malta – tel: 317088) operates a speedy catamaran service from Malta to Pozzallo (see page 18) with a journey time of one hour, 30 minutes. The UK agent for both the Gozo Channel Company and Virtu Rapid Ferries is Multitours, 21 Sussex Street, London, SW1V 4RR (tel: 071 821 7000).

Tour Operators

As a long-established holiday venue, especially for UK subjects, Malta has acquired much experience in catering for visitors, most arriving on 'package' deals which include the costs of return flights and accommodation (see page 30). Many tour operators also offer flights only and these are extremely popular with Maltese having family and other connections in the UK or elsewhere. Travel agents, newspaper advertisements and teletext provide information on bargain fares though the present state of the tourist market means that these are not nearly as common as they once were. The National Tourist Organisation of Malta (see page 20) provides an annually updated list of companies specialising in Maltese holidays. For 1990 this gave the addresses of 58 tour operators with information on the types of holiday they provided and details on the departure airports used by each company. The latter included Heathrow, Gatwick, Stansted, Luton, Birmingham, East Midlands, Manchester, Leeds/Bradford, Newcastle, Bristol, Exeter, Belfast, Southend, Cardiff, Edinburgh, Glasgow and Aberdeen.

Immigration and Customs

UK nationals require a valid passport, but no visa for a stay of less than three months. For visits in excess of this, applications should be made to the Immigration Police, Police Headquarters, Floriana. Should difficulties arise help and advice can be obtained from embassies and high commissions (see Practical Information).

There is no limit to the amount of foreign currency that can be brought into Malta, but large amounts should be declared on arrival, especially if there is a likelihood that much of it will be taken out again. The maximum amount of imported Maltese currency is LM 50 (50 Maltese Lira) and no more than LM 25 may be taken out. Foreign exchange facilities (see page 21) are available at Luqa Airport.

Clothing and belongings intended for personal use are not liable to import duty (but see note on car importation on page 11). The duty-free allowance for adults entering Malta is 200 cigarettes (or the equivalent in cigarillos, cigars or tobacco), one litre of spirits and one litre of wine, and a reasonable quantity of perfume, toilet water and gifts. Luqa's duty-free shop in the arrivals area will advise those in doubt. Passengers returning to the UK and other EC countries will usually have been issued with an information card on customs allowances.

TRAVEL ON MALTA

By Car

On both Malta and Gozo the short road distances between towns, villages and other venues of principal interest make touring by private car an attractive option and further bonuses are the relative cheapness of both petrol and car-hire rates. The latter, usually including unlimited mileage and insurance cover, are among the lowest in Europe, yet to quote current prices would be misleading for inflation, as in most holiday countries, is high. Private transport provides great ease and flexibility but, as noted below, driving on Malta is no sedative to the nerves and will not appeal to many visitors in search of a relaxing holiday. Those going to the trouble of bringing their own vehicles to Malta should formalise arrangements well in advance with the ferry companies mentioned above. On arrival they will be asked to sign a declaration to pay current import duties if the vehicle is locally sold.

CAR HIRE

In addition to international car-hire firms such as Avis, Hertz and Godfrey Davis, there are many reputable island companies and scores of small freelance agencies, though some of the latter are less reliable than others should motoring difficulties arise. Collectively, a wide choice of cars is available for hire by the day, week or month, the longer period arrangements proving the most financially favourable. Visitors should expect to pay more in peak tourist season and early booking is advisable. Most tour operators, as part of their package deal, can reserve cars at special rates for visitors on arrival, their local representatives also being adept in finding cars from reputable companies at short notice.

A valid British or International driver's licence is acceptable on Malta, though visitors hiring cars may be further asked to produce their passports. Maltese law allows driving from 18 years upwards with no upper-age limit. Most agencies, however, set the minimum and maximum car-hire age at 25 and 70, respectively. Here again tour representatives can often negotiate exceptions.

DRIVING CONDITIONS

Stories about island drivers and road conditions are now part of local folklore, and the cardinal rule for newcomers to this frenetic motoring experience is the exercise of patience and diligence at all times. Road accidents happen and visitors should carry, as in all unfamiliar situations, the telephone numbers of the police and ambulance services. This is not scaremongering, merely common sense and such important numbers for both Malta and Gozo should be checked as being operational, for code and other numerical changes can occur.

Throughout the islands walking is a dirty word and aversion to this type of physical exercise is reflected in the rapid annual growth of registered vehicles, particularly private cars, now estimated in the region of 120,000. A crude calculation based on a population of some 360,000 will provide a statistic of one car for every three people and visitors will quickly form the opinion that these converge at the same destinations at the same times.

PARKING

For obvious reasons the greatest scenes of traffic congestion are within the Valletta conurbation, though in most popular parts of the islands parking difficulties are acute. For the Maltese the narrow pavements in towns and villages – to the great inconvenience of pedestrians – are 'ideal' parking lots as are the STRICTLY NO PARKING areas and those demarcated as BUS STOP. Visitors will need to wrestle with their consciences as to whether or not they succumb to local example. Rare as the enforcement is, there are fines for illegal parking but the Maltese work on the principle that many legions of diligent traffic wardens would be needed to even scrape at the problem. Visitors, however, might well muse that just a week of rigorous fining might at least finance the foundations of further, much-needed multi-storey car parks.

MALTESE HIGHWAY CODE

An official one does exist and refers to the lawful speed limit of 40 kmph (25 mph) in built-up areas and 64 kmph (40 mph) on open roads. Other 'mandatory' rules closely follow those of the UK in that vehicles keep to the left, overtake on the right and at crossroads traffic approaching from the left-hand side has the right of way. At roundabouts (traffic circles) vehicles must give way to those entering from the right or to those already in the circuit. But all this is text-book theory which has been adapted by the Maltese to suit their own individualistic style and purpose. In summer, for example, the maxim seems to be to drive in the 'shade' whenever possible and another code of practice is that everybody has the right of way – except yourself. But, in fairness, some semblance of an organised pecking order has evolved in that priority is based on vehicle size, the aggressive-looking lorry (truck) or bus obviously having right-of-way over a van, and a van over a car, and so on down the line. Yet this workable principle is complicated by the Maltese obsession for speed, the fast 'yuppie' sportscar now challenging the lorry in this priority hierarchy. Not to be out-pointed, the motor-cyclists do everything to prove that they are the fastest vehicles on Maltese roads and with silencers removed the noisiest (another obsession) also. Weaving between traffic at dare-devil speed, further 'entertainment' is often provided by semi-acrobatic performances. Unfortunately such practice rarely makes perfect as the sad wayside shrines commemorating this folly testify.

ACCIDENTS

In the case of accidents the police must be called immediately and it is wiser not to move vehicles until they arrive, for insurance claims depend on an accurate, official report. In the event of breakdowns, those renting a car should first call the hire firm, the theory being that help will be sent within the hour. In high season this often means a towing service to the nearest garage rather than a replacement car. Malta has numerous garages and service stations, the latter closed on Sundays and public holidays, so visitors should be sure not to run out of fuel on Saturday night.

ROADS

Malta has some 1,300 kilometres of 'motorable' roads of various widths and in various states of repair. Though heavily congested those throughout the Valletta conurbation are of a reasonable standard and many large roundabouts and new traffic intersections have aided circulation, as have stretches of 'national' and 'regional' roads. Yet throughout the islands wider sections of highway can quickly become twisting country roads that pass through villages in a succession of narrow sharp corners. Other hazards are interminable road works, double-parked vehicles, roadside dumped building materials and uneven surfaces which further deteriorate into dangerous potholes.

The Maltese joke that they are fond of the latter, for they have grown up with them and are sad when repairs take place! This usually means a lethal infill of hot tar and a concoction of barely set chippings camouflaged with a dust topping.

MAPS

Signposting leaves much to be desired, the theory being that all Maltese know where they are going. A good road map is essential but recorded routes off main highways is no guarantee of easy or direct access to a particular destination. The circuitously disorientating country roads and lanes also have high walls and hedges which hinder visibility and novices to the island frequently get lost, though not for long. The domes and towers of parish churches provide some of the best landmarks and knowledgeable locals are adept in recognising their individual architectural features. Visitors heading for a church can be assured that its attendant village will have better directions to an intended destination.

Despite the otherwise informative quality of Malta's NTO brochures and fact sheets the free maps provided are basic in their information and of little use to visitors in search of the hidden parts of the countryside. But book-shops and news stands have a good choice of maps which indicate all main routes, the chief scenic and historical attractions and street plans of the Valletta conurbation, Rabat–Mdina and some of the newer resorts. By far the most useful map coverage is the 1 : 25,000 scale set which covers the islands in three sheets – Malta West, Malta East and Gozo and Comino. Produced in the 'sixties and reflecting the skills of the British Ordnance Survey, they are currently being updated by a French company and are invaluable for the walker and hiker.

By Bus

Those not wishing to drive and, nowadays, the few unable to do so (the author included!) will not be unduly inconvenienced, for Malta has an efficient bus service and fares are incredibly cheap. An added advantage is that the drivers know exactly where they are going, even when a series of unexpected detours prolongs what was expected to be a short 'crow-fly' journey. This is all part of the outing and visitors should be grateful for seeing, at no extra cost, villages and other places they might well have missed.

On Malta the departure and return point for what is a highly centralised system is the area surrounding the Triton

The Phoenicia Hotel and City Gate bus station

Fountain at Valletta's City Gate, this busy transport hub being administratively part of Floriana. Beneath their coverings of dust all public buses are coloured green and numbers only denote their destinations. Services are frequent with departure times ranging from five to 30 minutes, the former serving the Valletta conurbation and the main tourist resorts and the latter the island's more distant parts. Maltese drivers fully know the meaning of a 'busman's holiday' for there are few days of the year without scheduled services. Buses even run during the 'holy of holies', the often unbearably hot period of summer afternoons when all but 'mad dogs and Englishmen' – and a few other tourists besides – enjoy the siesta period in anticipation of the cooler temperatures to come. However from late afternoon onwards some services are restricted and enquiries should be made, especially about return times, at the Despatcher's Kiosk, City Gate. It has to be said that the usefulness of bus travel decreases with the distances visitors stay from City Gate and this is a factor which needs to be considered when choosing accommodation. As few service routes ignore the central terminus it can be time-consuming for those staying, for example, at Marsaxlokk who, wishing to visit Żurrieq and the Blue Grotto will need a bus to City Gate and a journey back to the south coast (and a return performance in the opposite direction). A few intermediate bus junctions simplify such procedures but the standard method is via City Gate (see p. 164 for main bus routes).

The Gozitan network operates from the main terminus in Victoria but services on the island are far less frequent and most run for the marketing convenience of the locals. Private transport is more of a necessity, for some buses leave the villages for Victoria at dawn and return as early as 10 am. Gozo's most regular services are timed to meet the Malta ferries, the buses leaving Mġarr for Victoria and in summer continuing on to the resorts of Marsalforn and Xlendi.

Bus travel is an integral part of Maltese life and an adventure no one should miss. The friendly drivers are true helmsmen of the roads and cater for many passenger needs, not least spiritual. The cramped driving area is decked out as a personalised shrine with holy pictures, family snapshots and such salient texts as 'In God we trust', 'Bless this journey', and 'Mother of God take care of us'. Maltese passengers reinforce these invocations by blessing themselves, the added security of this soon being appreciated as the horn-happy driver begins his onslaught on the island roads eager to reach his destination on time.

Icons and personal blessings serve other purposes, for most Maltese buses run on faith as well as on diesel. Although the Leyland fleet, now eons old and obsolete in most of Europe, is gradually being replaced by larger, plush-seated and roof-ventilated models, the network still relies on these charismatic bone-shakers which, for the omnibus connoisseur, are a privilege to ride on. Understanding his trusty steed with both affection and firmness, the driver is also an intuitive mechanic who works wonders on his vehicle with the sole aid of fist or boot. In addition to these duties he also takes the fares and despite the 'no change' stipulation amiably provides this down to the smallest of Maltese cents. Few would deny him his well-earned cigarette in a vehicle, for the comfort and safety of its passengers, he otherwise dutifully preserves as a STRICTLY NO SMOKING area.

Taxis

Though their reasoning is far from clear, the islanders claim that cheap bus travel is the cause of the high fares charged by Maltese taxis and many visitors pay excessive amounts for short distances. Taxis are clearly marked as such and also have red number plates. Their stands are found in most town squares, at the large hotels and at Luqa Airport and the ferry docks. Rates are officially regulated by the government and, by law, all cabs must have operational meters though it has become common practice that these are not automatically switched on or are deemed to be 'temporarily' out of order. In such cases the charge for a journey should be negotiated, especially at night when the last buses have gone. Wise to the problem, the Maltese phone the services of the 24-hour mini-cab firms whose standard rates are far more economical. The largest of these, Wembley Motors, is advertised everywhere.

The Ferries

There have been suggestions of linking Malta and Gozo by bridges using Comino as the intermediate stepping-stone. Financially expensive, though technically possible, the Gozitans, anxious to maintain their physical independence from Malta, have been ardent opposers of such a plan as have those eager to preserve the relative isolation and 'away-from-it-all' atmosphere of Comino. Currently, the only public link between Malta and Gozo is by ferry boat and the regular services (with telephone numbers for vehicle bookings) are advertised in the local daily newspapers. Disruption to schedules due to weather conditions or other causes is announced on the radio.

The large car ferry, *Għawdex*, leaves every morning from Sa Maison Pier in Pietà Creek and the journey time to Mġarr on Gozo is approximately one hour and 15 minutes. The air-conditioned passenger lounge and cafeteria makes this journey particularly relaxing and enjoyable. The *Melitaland*, a smaller and less expensive car ferry, leaves for Mġarr from Ċirkewwa on Malta's north-west coast. In summer it can be uncomfortably crowded but the advantages of this route are its frequent shuttle service (which in peak tourist season also operates throughout the night) and the short 20-minute journey time. The *Mġarr*, a more luxurious boat, also serves this route.

Comino can be reached by summer tour excursion boats from both Mġarr and Ċirkewwa, a 15-minute journey in either direction. This service is provided by the Comino Hotel though it is possible to reach the island by private agreement with Gozitan or Maltese fishermen. Travel agents also operate boats to Comino.

Gozo Air Link

A Malta–Gozo air link has been discussed. The problem is finding a suitable landing strip on Gozo and should a service come into operation it would be for small aircraft only, with seating for no more than twenty passengers.

Coach and Boat Excursions

Various travel agents offer a selection of sightseeing excursions to places of scenic and historical interest including

Gozo from Malta and vice-versa. These include evening, half-day and full-day trips, the latter usually including lunch in the tariff. It is worth shopping around for prices greatly differ between companies whose itineraries cover roughly the same ground. Few island tours verge off the beaten track and inevitably spend time at local tourist shops and handicraft centres, albeit of interest to those in search of presents and souvenirs.

Some of the most popular excursions are the boat trips that leave from The Strand, Sliema. Run by Captain Morgan and Jylland they include the Marsamxett and Grant Harbour cruise which visits the docklands and subsidiary creeks, and a full-day cruise around the coast of Malta. Visitors fascinated by the proximity of Sicily can avail themselves of two day excursions on Virtu Rapid Ferries which links Malta with Pozzallo, the crossing by luxurious catamaran taking 90 minutes. One tour visits Catania, the craters of Mount Etna and Taormina, and the other concentrates on the city of Siracusa (Syracuse) with its extensive Greek and Roman remains. From time to time sea trips run to Kelibia (Tunisia), situated on Cap Bon peninsula with relatively easy access to Tunis and the ruins of Carthage. These catamaran excursions are expensive and so are pleasure flights around the islands by Excelair. This company usefully operates a 24-hour air taxi service to destinations outside Malta.

Karrozin and Dgħajsa

These forms of conveyance, over short journeys only, are the ultimate in tourist transport. The *karrozin* is a quaint horse-drawn carriage introduced during the reign of Queen Victoria and its survival is due to tourist demand. It seats four people with a driver up-front and can be hired (fare negotiable) in Valletta, Sliema and Mdina. The height of the carriage gives a better view than from a car and a popular tour is around Valletta's bastions. Each horse usually has a pheasant feather stuck in its bridle, which brings good luck.

The *dgħajsa* (pronounced 'die-sah'), plural *dgħajjes* is a traditional colourfully-painted water taxi which is propelled by a standing boatman who pushes, not pulls, his long oars. Venetian gondolas are manoeuvered in a similar way and at Kalkara, where these craft are repaired, they are also called *gondla*, one theory being that they were introduced from Venice in the sixteenth century. But the eyes of Osiris, carved or painted on their bows make them essentially Maltese. Once used to ferry Royal Navy sailors from their anchored ships they can now be hired from Lascaris Wharf

A Valletta *karrozin* used for sightseeing

in Valletta or from the Senglea and Vittoriosa waterfronts. Prices need to be agreed with the *dgħajsaman* before embarking. These boats take part in a popular regatta held every September on the Grand Harbour.

Malta's other colourful craft are the fishing boats known as *luzzus*. For generations these have been painted in rich contrasting colours and have become something of a trademark for the islands. Finely painted scroll-work often decorates their bows, together with the protective eyes of Osiris.

PRACTICAL INFORMATION

Tourist Offices

Information on all aspects of Maltese tourism is available from the main office of the National Tourist Organisation of Malta (NTOM), Harper Lane, Floriana (tel: 224444). In addition branch offices are located at Luqa Airport (tel: 229915), Valletta (City Gate Arcade, tel: 227747), Sliema (Bisazza Street, tel: 313409) and St Julian's (Main Street, Balluta, tel: 342671). On Gozo there are offices at Mġarr harbour (tel: 553343) and in Victoria (Independence Square, tel: 556454). All provide free useful fact sheets, accommodation and other lists, maps and well-written colour brochures on the history, culture and landscape of the islands, together with entertainment, sporting and educational activities. Many of these publications are the result of Malta's contribution to the European Year of Tourism (1990) and are part of the NTOM's long-term tourism initiatives. In the UK the Malta Government Tourist Office is at College House, Suite 207, Wrights Lane, London, W8 5SH (tel: 071 938 2668).

The normal opening hours of tourist offices are 08.30–12.30 and 13.15–18.00 (Monday to Saturday) and 08.30–13.00 (Sunday). Times are more restricted on public holidays and some offices are closed. A tourism complaints officer has recently been appointed during office hours (tel: 605615) and a 24-hour answering service is due to be installed.

Embassies and Commissions

As an independent republic Malta has the embassies, diplomatic representations and cultural institutions of many world nations. They are listed in the telephone directory and information is also available from tourist offices. The British High Commission (tel: 233134–8) and the United States Embassy (tel: 623653) are both in St Anne Street, Floriana and the Australian High Commission (which has long dealt with Maltese emigrants) is at Airways House, Gaiety Lane, PO Box 8, Sliema (tel: 338201–5). In the UK the Malta High Commission is at 16 Kensington Square, London, W8 5SH (tel: 071 938 1712–6).

Police

Malta's Police Headquarters are in Floriana and all towns and tourist centres have police stations which are open day and night. They can be extremely useful for making emergency (only) calls abroad and the police are also responsible for delivering urgent messages to Maltese without telephones. Traffic police patrol the roads in cars or on motor-cycles and there are periodic speed checks and occasionally road blocks for identity purposes. But for most of the time Malta's police force maintains a low profile, though is quick to act when necessities arise such as a reported theft or motoring accident. Compared with many countries the islands are still relatively crime free and visitors are safe almost anywhere. The police are most vigilant in the control of drugs, their possession, use and sale being criminal offences. Spot searches can occur at discotheques or other suspected venues.

Currency and Banks

The currency is decimal and the monetary unit is the Maltese *lira* (LM). This is sometimes still referred to as the Maltese pound but its exchange value is not on a par with British sterling. One lira is divided into one hundred *centezmi* (cents) and ten *millezmi* (mils) make up a *centezmu*. Six liri, twenty cents and five mils is written as LM6.20.5. Banknotes are issued for 20, 10, 5 and 2 liri, the old 1 lira note being replaced by the 1 lira coin. Other coins are for 50, 25, 10, 5 and 1 cents, and for 5, 3 and 2 mils, though visitors confining themselves to the main towns and resorts will handle few of these.

The Central Bank of Malta issues the lira's official daily rates of exchange with foreign currencies and these are available from the main commercial banks. The largest, the Mid-Med Bank and the Bank of Valletta, have a network of offices throughout the islands. Though there are slight variations between winter and summer, banking hours are usually 08.30 to 12.30, Monday to Friday, and up to 11.30 on Saturday. In addition some banks in Valletta, Sliema, St Julian's and Buġibba provide foreign exchange services during the late afternoon period. Except for Christmas Day and New Year's Day the Luqa Airport exchange is open on a 24-hour basis but is available to incoming and departing passengers only. Most large hotels will exchange foreign currency though offering slightly lower rates. They are useful for obtaining money on Sundays and public holidays.

Eurocheques and traveller's cheques are widely accepted

and international credit cards can be used at most banks for obtaining cash. Many hotels, restaurants, travel agencies and shops accept plastic payment.

Post and Telephones

Malta's postal service is usually efficient. The General Post Office is at Auberge d'Italie in Valletta and all towns and many large villages have sub-post offices, though these are fewer on Gozo whose main post office is in Republic Street, Victoria. Stamps can be bought at most places where postcards are sold and UK visitors will have no difficulty in locating Maltese post boxes, for the majority are the familiar bright red rotundas or wall boxes with the insignia of British royalty, even including a few museum pieces with VR on them. The higher grade hotels have their own mail collections.

The telephone service is operated by the Telemalta Corporation and local calls are fully automatic. Many street corner telephone boxes are the old British kiosks, painted blue, and instructions are in Maltese and English. Cheap rates are available from 21.00–08.00, Monday to Saturday, and all day Sunday. Direct dialling is possible to most of western Europe and the USA and calls to other countries can be booked by dialling 994, but connections can involve a long wait. Should urgent overseas contact be necessary visitors are advised to use the new satellite telecommunications system at Telemalta's main office, Mercury House, St George's Road, St Julian's (tel: 338221 or 334041). Open 24 hours, this has telephone booths where individual calls are registered with an attendant to whom payment is subsequently made. The same system operates at the branch offices in Valletta, Sliema, Qawra and Luqa Airport, but office times are more restricted. Telemalta's main Gozitan office is in Republic Street, Victoria, and telephone calls can also be made from Marsalforn police station. Improvements to Malta's telephone service are being made all the time though it continues to be the subject of much criticism.

In theory a telephone call to the UK is easy. After inserting coins (LM1, 50c, 25c, 10c) the user will need to wait for the dial tone before proceeding with 044, followed by the UK area code (minus the initial 0), and the local number. For example to reach Winchester 841392 (area code 0962) the digital procedure would be 044 962 841392. Hotel guests will find telephoning from their rooms more convenient though this incurs substantially extra charges. Instructions for ringing Malta from the UK are given in the British Telecom Phone Book.

(Above) Spring fields, Marsaxlokk   (Below) Part of the rich Easter display, Mosta Church

(Left) Co-Cathedral of St John's, Valletta   (Right) Valletta's
Sunday market   (Below) Maltese boats, Spinola Bay

Time Differences

This is important when telephoning overseas. Malta follows Central European Time which is latitudinally one hour ahead of GMT. But from the last Sunday in March until the third Sunday in September the islands put their clocks forward by one hour, a beneficial move in terms of their 'summer' tourist trade. However, other countries alter their times, not least the UK and there is little international synchronisation of changeover dates. These equivalents provide a rough summer guide: when it is noon in Malta it is 06.00 in New York, 11.00 in London, 20.00 in Sydney and 22.00 in Auckland. New arrivals to the islands can always check the local time with Telemalta's speaking clock!

Newspapers

Visitors wishing further contact with the happenings at home can avail themselves of most major Western European newspapers, the UK selection ranging from *The Sun* and *News of the World* to *The Times* and *Daily Telegraph*. UK newspapers usually arrive on the day of publication, as do those from Italy, France, Germany and Libya. A number of local papers are published in Maltese and English, the most influential of the latter being *The Times* (of Malta), published daily. It carries all main international stories, as well as reports and articles of Maltese interest, providing the visitor with a better understanding of the political, economic and social issues currently affecting the country. The advertisements also provide useful information on eating places, entertainment, special events and ferry schedules etc. Its weekend equivalent, *The Sunday Times*, is a more voluminous newspaper and an exceptionally good read.

Radio and Television

Radio Malta's two services, RM 1 and RM 2, begin broadcasting at 06.00 and provide news, music and feature programmes until 23.00. There are regular news bulletins and other items in English. The BBC World Service is clearly heard and, usually, Voice of America broadcasts. Voice of the Mediterranean transmits daily in English and Arabic. Details and frequencies of all radio transmissions are given in local newspapers.

Malta is inundated by television channels, a factor of its location and the explanation of the forests of high roof-top aerials seen throughout the islands. As well as its own TVM channel it receives Italian national stations and local Sicilian

An old print showing country women at a well

networks, a choice of ten channels with more in the offing as satellite TV continues to grow in popularity. 'Tele-addicts' to the islands might well return with a basic smattering of Italian grammar.

Water

This is perfectly safe to drink though much of it is desalinated or heavily chlorinated, the fastidious claiming it taints the taste of tea and coffee. Some cafés advertise that their beverages are made from bottled water which is readily obtainable from corner shops and bars. There are still and naturally carbonated varieties, some brands imported from as far away as southern Ireland. Tap water should be used sparingly, especially in the parched summer months when it is one of Malta's most precious commodities. To conserve supplies mains water is sometimes turned off for periods, a roster system operating. Details of the localities affected are published in the daily newspapers and announced on the radio. Despite its scarcity, water management is such that personal and public hygiene is fully maintained.

Medical Care

The islands enjoy relatively high standards of health and medical care though the health service is short of money and there are long waiting lists for non-emergency treatment. St Luke's in Gwardamanga (part of the Valletta conurbation) is the main general hospital with all treatment departments, including casualty. Craig Hospital on Gozo is less comprehensive. In addition there are government-run clinics in other main centres and numerous local GP surgeries. The large hotels employ the services of an emergency doctor.

Reciprocal agreements between the Maltese and British governments allow for medical and hospital care and UK visitors are advised to take their NHS card. Those receiving medical treatment at home, carrying medicines into Malta or needing further local supplies should have a supporting letter from their family doctor. It is always wise to take out a full medical expenses insurance as some of the policies provided by tour operators are often limited in their cover.

The most common complaints afflicting visitors, especially in summer, are gastro-intestinal troubles and those induced by over-exposure to the powerful sun. These ailments are often linked and result from over-indulgence rather than poorly-prepared food or water quality. As noted below (page 48) the sun rules these islands for many months and obeying the sensible rule of gradual body exposure cannot be over-emphasised. A sun hat is often a necessary precaution as is walking in the shade (as the Maltese do) when the sun is its hottest. An occasional salt tablet is beneficial to those prone to excessive perspiration. Too much alcohol, successive late nights, exertion during the siesta period can, with a total change of diet, prove a sound recipe for illness and a partially ruined holiday.

Pharmacies

For many ailments a visit to the local pharmacy might be all that is needed, for Malta's pharmacists are qualified to give basic diagnostic advice and first aid. If unable to help they will refer customers to a doctor, dentist, or other specialist. All the well-known drugs, ointments and medicines are available on prescription and some over the counter. UK visitors will feel at home in Malta's chemists for many of them stock a large range of Boots' products – medicines, cosmetics, toiletries, perfumes and baby requisites including foods which are not generally available elsewhere. Pharmacies also stock a variety of sprays for insect bites and various aids that keep rooms free of flies, mosquitoes and other nuisances. But the fully prepared summer visitor will have purchased these before leaving, and highly recommended is the small and efficient electrical device known as 'Buzz-Off'.

Pharmacies are usually open from 08.00 to 13.00 and from 16.00 to 19.00. Some open longer on a roster basis and this changeable schedule includes Sundays. Newspapers publish this information and, in emergencies, the local police station will be able to help.

Electricity and Gas

Electricity supply is at 240 volts, single phase, 50 cycles and standard square-fitting, three-point British plugs should, theoretically, fit local sockets, though loose fittings are a common fault. Visitors from other countries will need adaptors and many hotels anticipate this need. Electrical faults do occur, often throughout entire districts, but rest assured, the hotel management or neighbours will be the first to contact the Malta Electricity Board.

The standard method of cooking in self-catering accommodation is by cylinder gas and this provision is usually efficiently maintained. Should supplies run out and the management be unavailable, local firms can quickly supply replacement cylinders as part of their 24-hour service.

Places of Worship

Malta is essentially a Roman Catholic country (see page 83) and there are many churches and chapels in every town, district and village. The majority of services are conducted in Maltese, but some churches, usually on Sundays and days of obligation, celebrate mass in English, French, Italian and German. Weekend newspapers and tourist guides carry details.

Malta's main Anglican communities worship at St Paul's Anglican Cathedral (Independence Square, Valletta) and Holy Trinity Church (Rudolphe Street, Sliema). St Andrew's Church of Scotland is in South Street, Valletta, and the Church of St George (Merchant's Street, Valletta) is Greek Orthodox. There are a number of Nonconformist places of worship, a synagogue and a prominent mosque which occupies Corradino Hill above Paola. The Salvation Army has long played a role in the religious and social affairs of Malta.

A street corner shrine in Valletta

National and Public Holidays

These are days when most services in Malta close down, but not bars, restaurants and places of entertainment (except on Good Friday). Also, as noted, buses keep going and taxis have some of their best days.

As well as the moveable religious feasts such as Easter the

following dates are Maltese holidays:

1 January	New Year's Day
10 February	St Paul's Shipwreck
19 March	St Joseph's Day
1 May	Worker's Day
7 June	'*Sette Giugno*' (commemorating the labour risings of 1919)
29 June	*Mnarja* Day (Feast of St Peter and St Paul)
15 August	Feast of the Assumption
8 September	Victory Day (celebrating Malta's successful offensives against the Turks and Axis Powers)
21 September	Independence Day
8 December	Feast of the Immaculate Conception
13 December	Republic Day
25 December	Christmas Day

The events and festivities associated with some of the days are detailed on pages 84–87. In addition, there are local parish *festi* celebrated throughout Malta and Gozo and the main carnival period held in February–March.

Property Purchase

Homes for sale to non-Maltese, especially Britons, has long been a feature of the local real estate market. Ten years ago two-bedroomed apartments and modest-sized villas were still relatively cheap, but with more financial investment coming into the country these 'homes in the sun' have rocketed in price, even old farmhouses in Gozo which need complete renovation. The property sections of Maltese newspapers also indicate the spate of new homes being built, many of them in apartment complexes. Some of the most sought after and expensive are along the Tower Road seafront in Sliema and many of the older and attractive stone houses have been sacrificed to the property speculators. It is common for new homes to be offered for sale in shell form which means that the purchaser is responsible for all the internal finishing and fittings, including kitchen and bathroom equipment. Buying a second or retirement home in Malta is no longer the financial attraction it once was. Timesharing exists, but it is a pale reflection of its counterparts in other Mediterranean areas. Those interested, however, will find that it is carefully and legally controlled and there are no touts that approach visitors with their hard-selling, special-offer techniques.

Business Information

Malta now sees its role as an important centre for trade, finance and business conferences. Information on investment can be obtained from the Malta Development Corporation in Valletta (tel: 221431). A major business event is the International Trade Fair, held from 1–15 July on a permanent site at Naxxar. Since it began in 1952 (then housed in San Anton Gardens) it has grown into a Mediterranean exhibition of major importance and has numerous foreign pavilions. The grounds also host a number of specialised trade fairs, including the Food and Drink Fair, the Furniture and Interior Decoration Fair, the Boat and Motor Fair and the Fashion and Accessories Fair. The other main exhibition venue is the Mediterranean Conference Centre, which is the refurbished Great Hospital of the Knights in Valletta. The NTO's annual 'Events Calendar' provides information on these and other activities.

HOTELS AND RESTAURANTS

Malta has accommodation to suit all tastes and pockets, offering everything from luxury international hotels to simple inns and guest houses. The amount of accommodation and also its general standard is expanding annually in response to both Malta's continuing importance as a vacation centre and growing role as a venue for Mediterranean conferences. An extremely useful booklet, published by the National Tourist Organisation (see page 20), is the yearly updated listing and categorisation of hotels, apartments, villas, guest houses and hostels. As well as quoting the bed capacity of each establishment – an important criterion for visitors wishing to choose either a busy or quiet holiday – it also provides telephone numbers and, where appropriate, telex, cable and FAX information. Each entry is further accompanied by a sequence of symbols indicating general and individual room services together with outdoor facilities and organised activities. The establishment's location, i.e., whether coastal or away from the sea, is also recorded.

Many tour operators have their own criteria for grading accommodation and because it is largely based on customer experience and feedback it provides another usually sound measure of standard. Those holiday companies specialising solely on Malta (many having locally-based head offices), are especially adept in arranging accommodation to suit the most individualistic of needs. However, visitors should note the necessity of advance booking especially if the intention is to holiday in Malta during the crowded late spring to early autumn period.

Hotels

Despite its popularity with day-time visitors, Valletta itself has few hotels or other types of accommodation but, as noted, the city can easily be reached from most parts of the main island. The largest concentration of hotels is in Sliema and its bustling western suburbs of St Julian's and St Andrew's – Paceville (Il-Qaliet). The other rapidly growing tourism zone and hotel centre is the northern coasts around Mellieħa Bay and, especially, the St Paul's Bay area where Buġibba has become Malta's nearest equivalent (though

Ornate wooden balconies run the length of this side façade of Valletta's Grand Master's palace

still diminuitively) of a Spanish 'costa' resort. Gozo's main concentration of hotels and other accommodation is at Marsalforn, an old fishing village which, like so many on the islands, now reaps greater financial benefits from its summer tourism.

Maltese hotels are categorised according to the internationally recognised star rating system and range in their levels of comfort and amenities from 5-Star (de luxe) to 1-Star (basic) establishments. This official grading is also numerically reversed with the superior standard hotels becoming those in the First Class category and the least refined falling into the Fifth Class grade (though the

accommodation offered in these is usually perfectly acceptable for short stays). The official classification can change
if, for example, the *Hotels and Catering Establishments Board*
deems that standards have fallen, though in Malta the
reverse trend is now the case with many refurbished hotels
moving upwards in the classification league.

Current NTO listings provide information on 124 hotels
with accommodation capacities of between 15 and 688 beds.
Their collective provision is for 17,381 guests and this
availability, together with the 12,951 beds in aparthotels
(see below) and holiday complexes, not counting guest
houses etc, stresses the major economic importance of
tourism to the islands. It also supports the fact that the
annual number of visitors to Malta far surpasses in size the
country's indigenous population.

More than two-thirds of these listed hotels belong to the
3- and 2-Star categories. They account for over 50 per cent
of bed capacity and are extensively used by the tour
operators. As a general measure of standard all 3-Star
establishments provide comfortably-furnished rooms with
private bath or shower facilities, internal telephones, radios
and, increasingly, televisions. They also have restaurant, bar
and lounge areas, and front office services operated on a 24-
hour basis. Some of the newly-built or refurbished establishments in this category have air-conditioning – often a
necessity in summer – but it is only the higher grade
categories that guarantee this provision. All 4- and 5-Star
hotels also have swimming pool facilities and/or private
beach or shore access. In addition they provide a variety of
sports facilities and night-time entertainment.

THE LUXURY HOTELS

Malta's oldest and most famous 5-Star hotel is the *Phoenicia*, located in Floriana close to Valletta's City Gate. Like
others in this de luxe category it belongs to a reputable
international chain, in this case *Trusthouse Forte* which also
has other interests in Maltese tourism. Built in the grand
style and surrounded by lush leisure gardens it has long
combined the elegance of the British–Maltese past with the
luxury requirements of the present. Currently it is undergoing complete refurbishment to match the 5-star holiday and
conference-hosting competition of the larger *Hilton International* and *Dragonara Palace* (both at St Julian's) and Malta's
latest addition to the de luxe list, the *Holiday Inn* at Sliema.
Not to be outdone, Gozo has its own 5-star hotel, the
Ta'Ċenc near Sannat. Smaller in capacity, this pool-centred
complex is of great character and there are many who rate its

facilities and services as the best on the islands. Though not attaining de luxe status the islands have 14 4-Star establishments many of them firm favourites with returning vacationers.

Apartments and Villas

Self-catering accommodation is a rapidly expanding area of Maltese tourism and most package tour operators offer a choice of apartments and villas in holiday villages and aparthotels. The latter are fully serviced apartment complexes which also offer a range of hotel facilities such as restaurants, bars, cafeterias and a variety of sporting and evening entertainment provision. Self-catering is especially convenient for families with young children and many of the larger complexes have child minding arrangements.

The NTO listings provide details on 14 First Class, 16 Second Class and 20 Third Class self-catering complexes, though others are in operation and await (because of their newness) official categorisation. The choice of self-catering accommodation ranges from the standard studio room to one, two and three bedroom apartments. All have sitting and/or dining areas, kitchens and bathrooms (or shower-rooms) and the majority have balconies. The largest complexes have capacities of 500–900 beds and, like their equivalents in Spain and elsewhere in the Mediterranean, have become the growth points for such ancillary services as mini-markets, souvenir shops, bars, restaurants and recreational amenities.

The main concentration of brochure-featured apartments and villas are at St Julian's–St Andrew's, and the areas around Mellieħa and St Paul's Bay, especially at Buġibba and Qawra. But self-catering accommodation is available throughout the islands and the travel sections of newspapers frequently carry advertisements for privately arranged lettings ranging from luxury residential apartments in Sliema to modernised farmhouses and other country properties. Many of the tour operators specialising in Maltese holidays also offer these more individualistic types of accommodation.

Guest Houses

These pensions-cum-boarding houses offer some of the cheapest accommodation on Malta and Gozo. They are the nearest Mediterranean equivalents of the UK's trusty 'B and B' establishments and Britisher's will most certainly experience *déjà vu* when confronted by a personable landlady, the wealth of plastic and ceramic bric-a-brac and, on occasions, a list of house rules. Names such as 'Southend', 'Lady Godiva', 'Sea Bank', 'Brighton' and even 'Fawlty Towers' further perpetuate the 'been here before' feeling. All reputable guest houses are officially listed by the NTO and of the 63 First and Second Class establishments, 30 have modest restaurant facilities, meals other than breakfast being additional to the standard daily charge.

The familiarity of guest house accommodation is recommended to visitors anxious to experience something of the Maltese 'at home' for few cater for more than 20 guests and the majority are family-run concerns. Most villages have at least one guest house and those distant from Valletta often glean part of their trade from visitors who have missed the last return bus to City Gate. The stranded should note that the cost of a night's accommodation in a Maltese guest house is often considerably cheaper than a late taxi fare from, for example, Rabat or St Paul's Bay to Sliema–Valletta.

Hostels

Malta is fully affiliated with the international Youth Hostels Association and information can be obtained from 17 Tal-Borg Street, Paola. In addition, church and student hostels provide inexpensive accommodation and details are available from NTO offices. The latter's listings recommend five hostels, two at First Class, which also provide meals (the *Marsaxlokk*, Żejtun Road, Marsaxlokk, and *St Francis Ravelin*, Floriana) and three at Second Class (the *Paceville*, 30 B Gale, Triq Wilga, Paceville; the *Trafalgar*, 100 Triq ic-Centurjur, Buġibba, and the *Youth Travel Circle*, Buskett, Rabat). Hostel accommodation is usually at a premium, especially at Paceville where beds are limited.

Restaurants

Most travel writers agree that recommending restaurants (as indeed hotels) is a hazardous business for places change, sometimes overnight, and in the case of eating establishments this is frequently the result of a change in chef. Suffice it to say that Malta has no scarcity of eating places and available meals range from those offered by the now prolific fast-food places to the extensive menus provided by the *haute cuisine* restaurants. New restaurants are opening all the time under the watchful eye of the *Hotels and Catering Establishments Board* whose strict official classification into four grades also determines the general level of prices

Queen Victoria presides over an open-air café in front of the Royal Malta Library in Valletta

charged. Some 130 first and second category restaurants are listed, many of which are in the higher-starred hotels and are open to non-residents. Regular tourist board publications including *Coming Events* and *What's On in Malta and Gozo* provide useful information on the choice of eating places.

As in most holiday venues full-and part-board visitors staying in lower grade hotels are usually confronted with standardised fares leaning heavily towards what is now termed 'tourist cuisine', dishes which cater (often somewhat unadventurously) for the collective palates of their international guests. Should gastronomical monotony prove to be the case, outside choice is readily at hand, the patronage level at lunchtime and in the evening often being a sound indication of a restaurant's quality and value for money. Restaurant meals are usually served from 12 noon to around 2.30 pm and from 7 pm until the late hours, especially in the main resorts and at weekends when many Maltese families eat out. The more upmarket restaurants increasingly specialise in Italian, French and Anglo-American cuisine but, more recently, the fares of Greece, Turkey and Arab countries have become available. The latest culinary choices in the Sliema–St Julian's area are restaurants serving Chinese, Japanese and Indian food, if somewhat tamed for western palates.

Much of the pleasure of holidaying abroad is trying local dishes though these are not readily available in many of the higher-starred hotels and restaurants. With this in mind visitors should not ignore the unpretentious, usually brightly neon-lit eating places in town backstreets, suburbs and villages. Their low official rating reflects their somewhat stark decor and restricted menu choice, rather than the quality of the food. Many are family-run concerns providing local specialities and as the islanders are good trenchermen extra-large portions are served at modest cost. Provided due warning is given many a cook will oblige with a local dish (see below) on request and seldom will visitors be disappointed.

LOCAL CUISINE AND PROVISIONS

Critics argue that there is no typical Maltese cuisine, the so-called 'traditional' dishes of the islands merely being hybrids of the culinary preferences of past rulers. Such a view obviously throws doubt on the national purity of any country's cooking and recipes, for where would Western Europe be (indeed the world) without the stalwart potato? Few would deny that Maltese gastronomy owes much to its history, but geography has also played a major role by dictating that local dishes are unmistakably Mediterranean in character with common ingredients such as tomatoes, onions, garlic, herbs, peppers and olive oil, the latter, however, sparingly used. Geography also explains why the strongest culinary influences emanate from Sicily and southern Italy, the varied pasta dishes with their rich sauces proving this point. But Malta is also a country of roast beef and two veg, and other British fare includes many immediately recognisable cakes and puddings such as apple pie.

Custard has less successfully bridged the cultural gap, at least in restaurants!

Those privileged to have been entertained by the Maltese at home will be left in little doubt as to the existence of a Maltese cuisine based on recipes handed down through generations. They will further appreciate not only the quality of the meal but also the lengthy, dedicated work that went into its preparation. For the cook, usually the housewife, the 'best' ingredients also mean the 'freshest' and in Malta supermarket shopping has been slow to catch on. The islands remain bastions of the produce markets and local shops and self-catering visitors will quickly find themselves apeing the morning shopping habits of the locals, and making friends in the bargain. General grocers and butchers open early, the latter offering fresh cuts of beef, lamb and pork, farm-reared chickens, rabbits and locally-prepared sausages (some extremely spicy) and other offal delicacies. The fishmongers compete, subject to availability, with a varied assortment of fresh catch, some recognisable to the visitor but others more exotic – swordfish, tunny, dentex and Malta's own fish, the lampuka, which is plentiful in late summer and autumn but unobtainable for the rest of the year. Prawns, octopus, squid and cuttlefish are usually available and often lobster, though this, as throughout the Mediterranean, is expensive.

From early morning onwards Malta's streets are alive with itinerant traders selling bread, milk, kerosene, fruit and vegetables. The latter's van or horse-driven cart is laden with fresh and (in season) cheap produce for the islands are largely self-sufficient in vegetables – potatoes, onions,

The daily horse-drawn produce cart is a common feature in villages and urban districts

tomatoes, peppers, cabbages, cauliflowers, marrows, beans and artichokes etc. Much of Malta's locally-grown fruit, however, is exported and that available at shops, markets and stalls is usually imported from Sicily, mainland Italy and Greece. When available visitors should try Maltese oranges, tangerines, melons, figs, mulberries and strawberries, making sure that all fruit is thoroughly washed before eating.

MALTESE SPECIALITIES

The brief descriptions that follow give some indication of the variety of authentic dishes available.

Soups: The basic Maltese soup is *Bradu* (broth) prepared from boiled beef flavoured with marrow (squash), turnip and celery. The fresh tomato soup is excellent as are various fish soups including *Aljotta*, a highly seasoned dish with mixed herbs and onions. A challenge to the fastidious is *Qarnita*, a thick cuttlefish and octopus concoction with onions, olives, nuts, raisins, tomato purée and wine. Popular during Lent is *Soppa ta'l-Armla* ('Widow's Soup') which is more of an egg and cheese stew with cauliflower, peas and herbs. But by far the most popular Maltese soup is *Minestra*, the equivalent of *minestrone*, though its contents are bulkier and include all kinds of vegetables and a thick helping of pasta. *Kawlata* is a variant made from boiled pork with generous quantities of broad or haricot beans. Most soups, especially in country areas, are meals in themselves and are usually accompanied by fresh crusty Maltese bread.

Fenek dishes: Rabbit (*fenek*) is a Maltese speciality and these animals are often home reared, their meat being especially popular on festive occasions. Rabbit stew is something of a national dish, the meat first being fried in oil and red wine before casseroled with vegetables, herbs, garlic and more wine. This delicious dish with its rich gravy is usually served with boiled potatoes and cauliflower. Rabbit meat is also roasted or served in a pie – *Torta tal-fenek* – with a crusty top and baked with pieces of pork, vegetables and herbs.

Pasta and rice dishes: Of Malta's variety of pastas *Timpana* is a great favourite and also the most filling. Rarely is it available in restaurants for it carries the stigma of a 'peasant dish', though it is eaten by everyone. Made with a long, thick type of macaroni mixed with liver, vegetables, hard and soft eggs and other ingredients that come to hand, this embryonic pie is then encased in pastry and cooked to produce a dish capable of appeasing most appetites. Equally substantial is *Ravjul*, a Maltese equivalent of *ravioli*, the

The Neptune Court in the Grand Masters Palace

(Above) Dockyard Creek and Vittoriosa   (Below) Limestone
countryside along the Victoria Lines

Victoria Cathedral, Gozo

filling being *ricotta* which is a cottage cheese made from sheep's milk. The dish is covered with a richly aromatic sauce and parmesan cheese. The Maltese also indulge in an assortment of *risottos*, that known as *Ross fil-Forn* being a savoury rice cooked with mincemeat, eggs, peppers, tomatoes and grated cheese.

Stuffed vegetables: Freshly stuffed vegetables such as peppers, marrows, aubergines and globe artichokes are other meals in themselves and as well as being a standby of the Maltese housewife they often appear on restaurant menus. Their fillings consist of mixtures of seasoned mincemeat, onions, tomatoes, parsley, olives, breadcrumbs and anchovies, depending on the vegetable involved. Some of these dishes are dressed with sliced potatoes and semolina before cooking.

Lampuka pie: The seasonal nature of this fish has already been noted, so when lampuka dishes are available they have to be tried, especially the delicious *Torta tal-Lampuka*. Slices of this enigmatic fish are first seasoned and fried before being placed on a bed of pastry together with a mixture of tomatoes, onions, parsley, capers, peas and cauliflower, the dish then being sealed with more pastry and baked. A less complicated recipe is lampuka alone, cooked in pastry and served with vegetables and/or a side salad.

Bragioli: This is Malta's variant of 'beef olives' and another speciality. It is made of thin slices of steak on top of which is spread a mixture of minced bacon or ham, olives, parsley and garlic, bound together with breadcrumbs and beaten egg. The meat slices are then rolled up and simmered in a stock laced with onions and wine.

Desserts: As noted, Britain has a strong influence on Maltese puddings, but so has Italy with its tradition for mouth-watering ice-creams and sorbets (see below). Some of Malta's authentic desserts appear only during *festi* or at carnival time. Such is *Prinjolata*, an elaborate pyramidal concoction of sponge fingers held together by an almond-flavoured cream, melted chocolate and topped with cherries. More readily available is *Kannoli*, flour cornets filled with sweetened *ricotta* and, if lucky, visitors will come across various sweetmeats made from local honey. Some type of fresh fruit is always in season and, accompanied by local cheese, provides a delicious conclusion to any meal. The most popular cheese is *Gbejna*, a Gozitan speciality made from goat's milk and available fresh (*friski*), half-dried (*moxxi*) or peppered (*tal-bzar*).

Snacks and refreshments: Visitors in search of a lighter meal are well catered for in the main towns and tourist areas. Most bars carry a range of snacks and the cafés usually have extensive menus, especially the large open-air ones which are popular meeting places for Maltese and tourists alike. Pizzerias are now ubiquitous and their wide variety of toppings carry both traditional and Maltese names such as 'Margherita', 'Four Seasons', 'Marinara' and 'Capricciosa'. These busy establishments often offer an additional tempting range of pastas. Other international 'fast-food' fares include hot-dogs and hamburgers, a more recent innovation being the availability of Turkish-style kebabs and souvlakia. A typical Maltese snack is *Patizzi*, a flaky pastry filled with a mixture of *ricotta*, onions, peas and (usually) anchovies. As a mid-morning snack the locals buy it fresh, crisp and hot from corner kiosks or street vendors.

For the ultimate in ice-cream pleasure the main towns and resorts have their popular *Gelaterias* where the choice of frozen flavours on offer is legion. In case there is any doubt most bars serve coffee and the majority of cafés are licensed for alcoholic drinks. In addition to many international beers and lagers (some on draught) Malta has its own brands brewed by Farsons (Simonds Farsons Ċisk Ltd). Hopleaf and Blue Label ales and Ċisk (pronounced 'Chisk') lager are extremely good. Under franchise Farsons produces many international soft drinks but an alternative to Schweppes and the Colas is its own *Kinnie*, a bittersweet thirst-quencher made from oranges and herbs. The busiest bars have a bewildering selection of spirits, liquers, vermouths and sherries etc, but those used to the generous measures of Spain and other Mediterranean countries should note that shorts in Malta are served from optics. The British are to be blamed for this!

Compared with the imported vintages the local wines are cheap and range from light table varieties to those with a high alcoholic content. Few pretend to be the connoisseur's choice though quality has greatly improved since Malta's wineries have become more scientifically managed. In view of the modest outlay for a generally palatable bottle few would take exception to slight variations in brand quality. Among the local names offering both reds and whites are *Lachryma, Vitis, Farmers, Marsovin Special Reserve* and *Mistra Special*. Gozitan wines such as *Velson* and *Ġgantija* are the most potent and deserve respect.

GEOLOGY AND CLIMATE

The most striking feature of the Maltese landscape is its stony character, the main cause of which is the limestones that form most of the bedrock of the islands. These outcrop at the surface in rugged escarpments and rock-bound valleys, and reach the coast as high craggy cliffs and marine-etched headlands that shelter coves and larger bays. Being pervious rocks (allowing water to pass through them), the limestone areas are dry and large parts of the islands support a generally thin and infertile soil. The best farmlands occur on the richer soils of the moisture-retentive clays but these are limited in their extent, especially on Malta itself.

The limestones are the time-honoured building materials (see below) of the islanders and in the countryside the ubiquitous dry-stone walls that bound lanes, fields and terraced slopes add to the landscape's general stony appearance. Viewed from a distance it is often difficult to distinguish them from the natural bedrock on which they stand. Farmsteads, villages and the rapidly expanding towns are also predominantly limestone built and subtly blend in colour with the natural environment, especially in summer when the islands are at their driest and look most barren. Both as natural outcrops and as fashioned stone – monumental or otherwise – the limestones weather on exposure to a pale yellowish-brown colour and in the hot and glaring summer sunshine buildings and rock exposures alike take on a 'honey-glow' appearance. It would be romantic to suggest that 'Melita' – the early name for Malta (from the Greek word *meli*, that is, 'honey') – has its origins in this distinctive feature of the Maltese landscape. However, there are other suggestions as to Malta's meaning (see page 68).

Summer visitors might easily conclude that much of the countryside is little more than bare, parched ground, but closer inspection will reveal a wealth of small-scale landscape contrasts and visual surprises. The walls and hedges hide and protect valuable pockets of intensively cultivated land which, like the countryside in general, quickly responds to seasonal weather changes (see pages 48–50). The landscape enthusiast will soon appreciate that, rather than uniformity, the Maltese scene presents a complex pattern of frequently changing shapes and colours, the visual summary of centuries of human adaptation to these stony islands.

The Geological Sandwich

All of Malta's rocks belong to the general type known as *sedimentary* which means they were deposited in geological seas or large water basins as sediments worn away from ancient land masses. Varying physical and climatic conditions controlled the composition and thickness of these deposited layers (*strata*) which, in the process of time, became compacted and hardened to produce the local stratigraphical sequence. These also became folded and faulted (see below) by earth movements, a major cataclysm (or series of them), together with rises in sea level, severing the land bridges which once linked the islands with Sicily and Italy. Fossil evidence supports this theory as does the relative shallowness (less than 100 fathoms) of the Strait of Messina and the channel now separating Malta from Sicily.

Malta's sedimentary rocks, young in terms of the geological record, belong to the period of time known as the *Cenozoic* era which began about 70 million years ago. This

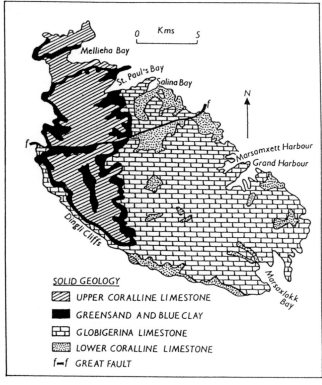

SOLID GEOLOGY

- ▨ UPPER CORALLINE LIMESTONE
- ■ GREENSAND AND BLUE CLAY
- ▦ GLOBIGERINA LIMESTONE
- ▩ LOWER CORALLINE LIMESTONE
- f—f GREAT FAULT

Malta's geology

is subdivided into the earlier *Tertiary* period, to which Malta's bedrocks belong, and the *Quarternary* period which began about two million years ago. For the latter, 'deposits' is a better name than 'rocks' and on Malta this most recent of geological periods is represented by river gravels and 'deposits' that have accumulated in limestone caves and along the coasts. The *Cenozoic* is also called the 'Age of Mammals' and the fossil evidence indicates that as the era progressed into *Quarternary* times the 'Age of Man' is reached. As yet, there is no evidence to prove that the Maltese Islands were inhabited by Palaeolithic (Old Stone Age) peoples, though cave discoveries (see page 61) trace the record back to later Stone Age times, approximately 5,000 years BC.

From the oldest rocks to the youngest, Malta's geological sandwich consists of Lower Coralline Limestone, Globigerina Limestone, Greensand and Blue Clay and Upper Coralline Limestone. The Coralline beds take their name from the many coral fossils they contain and they can be regarded as the 'crusts' of the sandwich which has a 'filling' of softer rocks between them. On exposure they weather and harden to provide durable building materials especially resistant to the corrosive effects of sea spray and salt-laden winds. They were frequently used by the Knights in the construction of their great coastal forts and other defences and some have argued that, without this stone, Malta would never have become the great military fortress it did.

The Globerigina Limestone is also named after its fossil composition, the minute shells of protozoa which make up this thick limestone series which covers some two-thirds of Malta. It also indurates on exposure, though it is a softer rock than the Corallines and can easily be cut (the Maltese liken it to hard cheese) and chiselled. It was an important building material for the sculptures and other architectural embellishments of the Baroque and later churches, palaces and public buildings. More prone to erosion the lower storeys of buildings in this limestone are frequently colourwashed for protection.

The islands have some huge stone quarries and visitors will see fields where the cut cubic blocks are stacked ready for use. But output barely keeps pace with the current construction boom and as quarries are worked out, or become otherwise uneconomic, new ones are opened. Many have been reclaimed for farming purposes.

Topography

The main island has a land area of only 246 square

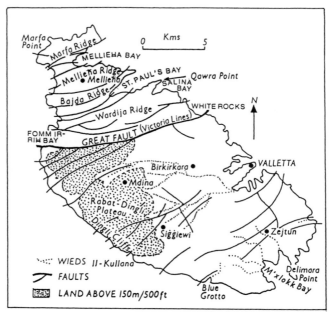

Malta's topography

kilometres and measures 27 kilometres at its longest (from Marfa Point in the northwest to Delimara Point in the south-east) and 14 kilometres at its widest (from Qawra Point on the north coast to Il-Kullana on the south). Yet within this small confine, where land reaches no higher than 253 metres (829 feet), the topography is varied, not least around the island's irregular coast which covers a distance of 137 kilometres. The main relief variations are caused by faulting, fractures in the 'rock sandwich' along which vertical or horizontal movements (sometimes both) have taken place. Many of these zones of weakness were initiated by the above-mentioned earth movements but in more recent times geological instability has been abetted by the tremors and eruptions of Sicily's Mount Etna, its 3323-metre summit sometimes visible from Mdina's ramparts and other parts of the island. Europe's largest, and one of the world's most active volcanoes, Etna's recorded periods of activity (the most recent being 1928, 1950–1, 1971 and frequent tremors in the 1980s) have more than registered on Malta. Each tremor physically 'lubricates' the complicated fault pattern that slices the island from northeast to southwest and the least of the troubles are landslips that affect the less-consolidated rocks.

In the northwest, faulting has thrown Malta's rocks into

a series of parallel limestone-capped ridges such as Marfa, Mellieħa, Bajda and Wardija. These craggy, fissured and cave-infested outcrops rise, respectively, to 122 m (400 ft), 145 m (475 ft), 84 m (175 ft) and 143 m (470 ft), and separating them are down-faulted depressions which have accumulated a deep downwash soil cover eroded from the bounding ridges. These provide Malta with some of its most fertile farmlands, especially the Pwales Valley between the Bajda and Wardija Ridges. Where the fault pattern reaches the coasts, the sea has etched a complex series of rugged headlands and large indentations, especially along the east coast where Mellieħa, St Paul's and Salina Bays bite deeply into the land.

THE GREAT FAULT

Rising to 239 metres (785 feet), Malta's most prominent escarpment is caused by what the geologists refer to as the Great Fault. Crossing the island from the vicinity of the White Rocks on the northeast coast to Fomm ir-Riħ Bay in the southwest, its steep north-west-facing edge is cut by ruggedly dry stream courses and a series of *cols* or gaps which take the names Naxxar, Targa, Falka, Binġemma and Santi. These now provide routes for the main roads linking the northwest with the remainder of the island. But the major historical role of this escarpment has been its defensive value to that area of Malta to its south and east, this defended boundary often ignoring the needs of the northwest by leaving it isolated and vulnerable to corsair attacks. Despite the fertility of its valleys this has resulted in a sparse population and frequently abandoned settlements, only to be reoccupied in more settled times.

The Knights recognised the defensive merits of the Great Fault and built watchtowers along its crest, but it was the British who systematically strengthened it (from 1875 onwards) with forts – Madliena, Mosta and Binġemma – batteries and entrenchments. These were collectively called the Victorian Lines (by which name the ridge is known today) and the defences suggest that the military experts of Victorian Britain were in accord with the Knights in regarding northwest Malta as tactically expendable. Even so, considerable nineteenth-century resettlement resulted, especially in and around the villages of Mġarr and Mellieħa and today the northwest is one of Malta's major tourism growth-points.

THE RABAT-DINGLI PLATEAU

Adjoining the south-western part of the Great Fault is

Malta's main area of elevated land. Referred to as the Rabat–Dingli Plateau, its surface rock is largely Upper Coralline Limestone with some more fertile pockets eroded into the underlying Greensand–Blue Clay. It reaches the sea in a lengthy protective western wall of high cliffs some with sheer drops to the inhospitable shore, Malta's highest point being close by. The plateau's eastern edge is fretted by a series of entrenched valleys whose intervening spurs have always provided good defensive sites. Mdina, the ancient and medieval capital, occupies one of these spurs and commands extensive views over a large part of the island. Such positions were also favoured as sites for some of the main knightly palaces that gravitated to the countryside, for example, the Verdala and Inquisitors Palaces.

THE GLOBERIGINA 'LOWLANDS'

Away from the Great Fault and the Rabat–Dingli Plateau the remainder of Malta largely consists of Globerigina Limestone forming countryside which, in a general fashion, slopes from west to east. Where not urbanised or providing land for airfields it is devoted to agriculture which supports a large number of rural villages and townships. 'Lowlands', however, is a misnomer for the countryside is cut by a complicated pattern of steep, rocky valleys known locally as *wieds*, a derivative of the Arabic word *wadi(s)*. Also characteristic of other parts of the islands, these are generally dry except after periods of heavy rainfall when, for a short time, they can become torrents capable of destructive land erosion, especially of the terraces and other pockets of farmland that utilise their sides.

In the Mdina area Wied il-Hemsija and Wied Incita join to become Wied is-Sewda and, to the south, Wied ta'l Isqaf, Wied il-Luq and others become Wied ir Kbir which joins Wied is-Sewda to enter the Grand Harbour via Marsa Creek. Together with Marsamxett Harbour and the other tributary creeks, the Grand Harbour is the drowned estuary of an ancient drainage system, these deep water provisions allowing Malta to serve as a major naval base throughout much of its history. The other main system of *wieds* is directed towards the large bay of Marsaxlokk which bites deeply into Malta's southeast coast. This, too, has played its naval and, nowadays, merchant role in the fortunes of the islands.

The bluffs between the *wieds* are the main sites for the older Maltese villages and townships – the *casals* (see page 84). Elevation offered them protection from flash-flooding and vantage points over the countryside in times of danger.

But the other controlling factor in their distribution was the availability of a trusty water supply either from freshwater springs or deep wells. This has been a crucial element in rural life and water tanks and other storage devices are common countryside features. The larger reservoirs are the products of the British and recent eras.

Gozitan Contrasts

The short stretch of sea from Ċirkewwa on Malta to Mġarr on Gozo, a crow-fly distance of some 5 kilometres, is divided by the island of Comino into the North and South Comino Channels. Together with its tiny and uninhabited acolyte, Cominotto, these islands cover an area of only 2.6 square kilometres. Both are largely composed of Upper Coralline Limestone which accounts for their rocky, water-less and cliffed appearances (see page 158).

Gozo is little more than one-quarter the size (67 square kilometres) of Malta and measures 14 kilometres at its longest (from Dimitri Point in the west to Qala Point in the east) with a maximum north–south width of 7 kilometres. The rock sequence is identical to Malta's, but Gozo's erosional history has led to many points of difference which are reflected in topographical details. The island has more extensive outcrops of Blue Clay, providing it with water-retentive soils and fertile farmlands which have adequately sustained the Gozitans and frequently supplied Malta in times of deficiency. One of the main contrasts with Malta is

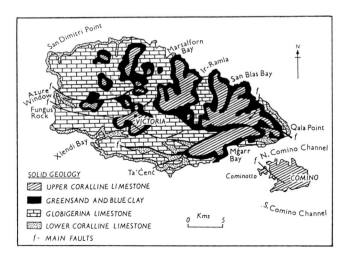

Gozo's geology

the greener appearance of the landscape, the other being its hillier nature, for the island is dominated by a series of table-shaped, 'mesa-like' elevations. Though few rise much above 150 metres (500 feet), the deep valleys separating them intensify the hilly character. Less faulted than Malta, these flat-topped Gozitan summits are capped by Upper Coralline Limestone and are the main locations for settlement including the central capital, Victoria (Rabat).

Though essentially rugged, Gozo's coastline (measuring 43 kilometres) is less indented than Malta's and the only port, except for small fishing harbours, is Mġarr. This has meant that the Gozitans have traditionally relied on farming and fishing, leaving trading and other maritime contacts with the rest of the world to the instincts of their neighbours on the main island.

Large sections of Gozo's coast are not accessible by road, but for the walker there are numerous impressive sights. These include (see page 146) the Azure Window, the Inland Sea, Dwerja Point and Fungus Rock in the west, and the Ta'Ċenc cliffs in the south which rival those of Dingli.

LANDSCAPE NAMES

Many of Malta's place names are highly descriptive, especially of the character and features of the countryside. Some frequently occurring place name elements of interest to the landscape enthusiast are the following: *aħrax* (rugged), *baħar* (sea, bay), *bir* (well), *blata* (rock), *borġ* (tower), *bur* (meadow), *gebel* (rocky hill, summit), *għajn* (spring), *għar* (cave), *ġnien* (garden, orchard), *ħal* or *raħal* (village or small town), *kbir* (large, great), *marsa* (harbour, inlet), *nadur* (look-out point), *qala* (bay, cove), *qortin* (promontory), *ramla* (sandy bay), *ras* (headland), *rdum* (cliff), *tarġa* (gap), *wied* (dry, rocky valley) and *xagħra* (waste or rocky area).

Climate

The landscape character of the islands, as indeed the entire pace of Maltese life, greatly varies in response to the seasonal differences of what is held to be a classic Mediterranean climatic regime. Simply stated, this is one of mild wet winters, hot dry summers and, for a large part of the year, clear blue skies and a high intensity of sunshine. Yet it would be misleading to suggest that Malta's climate can be predictably divided into two main seasons lasting from November to April and from May to October, respectively. Such a clinical classification obviously oversimplifies the detail of seasonal weather sequences, especially at the main

Average temperatures and rainfall

month	average air temperature minimum °C	minimum °F	maximum °C	maximum °F	average sea temperature °C	°F	average hours of sun	average rainfall in mm	average number of rain days
Jan	9.5	49	15.0	59	14.5	58	5.3	88.2	13
Feb	9.4	49	15.4	60	14.5	58	6.3	61.4	10
Mar	10.2	50	16.7	62	14.5	58	7.3	44.0	8
Apr	11.8	53	18.7	65.5	16.1	61	8.3	27.5	5
May	14.9	59	23.0	73.5	18.4	65	10.0	9.7	3
Jun	18.6	65.5	27.4	81.5	21.1	70	11.2	3.4	1
Jul	21.0	70	30.2	86.5	24.5	76	12.1	0.9	1
Aug	21.8	71	30.6	87	25.6	78	11.3	9.3	1
Sep	20.2	68.5	27.7	82	25.0	77	8.9	44.4	4
Oct	17.1	63	23.7	75.5	22.2	72	7.3	117.9	7
Nov	13.8	57	19.9	68	19.5	67	6.3	75.5	11
Dec	11.1	52	16.7	62	16.7	62	5.2	96.0	14

changeover periods when the islands experience seasons, albeit sometimes short, of spring and autumnal weather. Both provide ideal conditions for visitors interested in active sightseeing and walking holidays.

The accompanying table summarises monthly conditions and is based on averages taken over a period of at least thirty years. It indicates the high temperatures from May to October, four of these months also having negligible rainfall totals. As the number of rain days column suggests, precipitation during these months is caused by rare, short-lived thunderstorms. What these average temperaure figures fail to register is the intense summer heat sometimes experienced on the islands. Temperatures can soar in excess of 32°C, particularly when the *Sirocco* blows from North Africa, its moisture-absorbing sea journey also causing high humidity levels. *Xlokk* is the Maltese name for this enervating wind which can cause dizziness and other bodily troubles, and it is capable of parching summer crops in a short space of time. Fortunately its most intensive form is not a frequent occurrence, but visitors should be wary of all summer winds, even the deceptively benign land and sea breezes which locally cool the atmosphere though fail to temper the sun's powerful and harmful ultra-violet rays.

Malta's summer climate is dominated by the high pressure systems that persist throughout the Mediterranean basin. By late September these are increasingly challenged by cooler air depressions encroaching from continental Europe or eastwards from the Atlantic. They bring rain in the form of short-lived storms, especially in October (Malta's wettest month) when heavy downpours can cause great damage and soil erosion in the countryside. The weather then frequently calms into what the Maltese call St Martin's Summer (the equivalent of an 'Indian Summer') with warm, sunny and showery days. This is an ideal visiting time for those averse to excessive heat and the Maltese 'autumn' is a period of busy farming activity and the resurrection of plants that lay dormant throughout the drought months.

From the end of November onwards the Maltese climate is essentially unpredictable, the air mass conflicts producing day-to-day weather scenarios as complex and variable as those of the UK winter. Days of low cloud, drizzle and persistent rain can alternate with warmer and often extended sunny periods. The prevailing winds are now usually from the north and answer to such local names as *majjistral* (north-westerly), *tramuntana* (northerly) and *grigal* (north-easterly). The latter, also known as the Mediterranean *gregale*, is a particularly boisterous wind credited with causing many coastal disasters, not least St Paul's shipwreck (see page 69). It often blows into the confines of the Grand and Marsamxett Harbours, thus impeding their use to shipping. The long breakwater leading to St Elmo lighthouse at the entrance to the Grand Harbour was built to resist its ravages. Life on the islands is heavily dependent on the rain brought by these northerly winds but even this is not assured. A change in air mass direction causing winds to come up from the south can lead to infrequent showers only and major water shortages. Hence to quote the average annual rainfall total of the islands as 578 mm has very little meaning in view of the variations that occur from year to year.

Winter rainfall amounts determine the character of the Maltese countryside in spring, a time when the islands are usually at their greenest and fields and hillsides are colourfully carpeted with a profusion of wild flowers. Through to the end of May temperatures are pleasantly warm with nights on the cool side, and many regard spring as the best time for visiting the islands. There is the added bonus of the Maltese celebrations leading up to and including Easter.

NATURAL HISTORY

Plant Life

Malta's flora is the product of many factors, not least the climate of the islands which ensures drought conditions for the main summer months. Aridity is further increased by the predominantly limestone geology and these conditions limit natural plant species to xerophytic (drought resisting) communities. Equally – though many would argue of greater importance – has been the effect of centuries of human interference as successive people have cleared the indigenous vegetation cover to provide fuel, building materials and land for cultivation and settlements. Added to this has been the ruthless policy of overgrazing by sheep and, particularly, the voracious goat. Not only has this caused further destruction it has also prevented natural regeneration, thus intensifying the acute problem of soil erosion.

TREE SPECIES

It appears that climatic change has also played a part in the development of Malta's vegetation cover. The suggestion is that the islands were wetter places in prehistoric times when the early agriculturalists (see page 58) occupied a land with a good soil and woodland or tall shrub cover. Pollen studies have revealed the presence of species such as ash and hawthorn (now largely relegated to more northerly latitudes) and the leguminous Judas Tree (*Cercis siliquastrum*) which is still common throughout the islands. Its pink–purple flowers bloom in spring before the leaves appear and it is a salient herald to Easter for this is traditionally the tree on which Judas Iscariot hanged himself after betraying Christ.

But the most prominent species in Malta's early woodland cover appears to have been the holm oak (*Quercus ilex*), a useful tree throughout the Mediterranean. Since early times it has been used as a hard durable timber, in house- and ship-building, and for underground construction because of its resistance to decay. In addition it provided a high quality charcoal and its acorns, as of other oaks, were valuable pig fodder. Small surviving pockets of these oaks can be seen in the Mġibah Valley (between St Paul's and Mellieħa Bays), in the neighbourbood of Wardija (south of

St Paul's) and at Buskett (south of Rabat) which is Malta's largest conserved wooded area and once a hunting ground for the Knights.

Reference to indigenous trees are preserved in island place names such as Għajn Snuber on Malta's north-west coast. It means 'spring of the Aleppo pine' and though no species have survived in the locality, stands of this stately tree (*Pinus halepensis*) occur throughout the islands, the majority planted for ornamental purposes and often reaching 20 metres in height. Its timber was also widely used for house- and ship-building and the resin it provided was the basis of many medicines and preservatives. The carob or algarroba (*Ceratonia siliqua*), another native tree, is otherwise known as the Locust Tree for its pods are thought to be the 'locusts' eaten by John the Baptist and its dried husks those that sustained the Prodigal Son. Certainly the carob has helped to feed many a family in times of need and its husks are nowadays stored as animal fodder. The sticky juice of its ripe pods has been used for making syrups and fermented drinks.

Other Mediterranean trees and large shrubs common to Malta, and both widely naturalised and cultivated, are the almond (*Prunus amygdalus*), fig (*Ficus carica*), sweet bay (*Laurus nobilis*), olive (*Olea europaea*) and common vine (*Vitis vinifera ssp. sylvestris*). The tamarisk (*Tamarix*), with its feathery grey-green leaves and delicate pink spring flowers, is found in sandy coastal areas. It is often associated with the chaste tree (*Vitex agnus-castus*), traditionally believed to be a preserver of chastity. Also called 'Abraham's balm' it has small scented lilac or blue flowers which in summer are carried on long terminal spikes like a miniature buddleia.

Because of its central Mediterranean position Malta has acquired many now acclimatised species from other shores, not least the lofty date palm which most probably arrived from Tunisia. Malta's dates, however, hardly ever ripen, the islanders having more success with oranges and other cultivated fruits.

MAQUIS AND GARIGUE

By far the most characteristic plant associations on the islands are the mixed scrub communities known as *maquis*. They are the result of secondary colonisation of land cleared of its original vegetation or long abandoned farmlands that have reverted to the wild. *Maquis* consists of a tangled growth of drought-resistant and frequently aromatic plants and bushes, where one species rarely dominates and few grow in excess of one metre in height. Many have spikes and prickles rather than leaves (a drought-resisting ploy) and for the poorly-shod walker the *maquis* proves to be one of the main hazards of the Maltese countryside. On the more rugged limestone exposures, with the thinnest of soil coverings, a further state of degeneration is reached in the *garigue*, capable of supporting only the sparsest and most stunted of plants.

But these scrublands are areas of great beauty, for with the first burst of rain they miraculously turn ablaze with colour. Many of the semi-dormant plants are bulbous and tuberous species, the wild ancestors of the cultivated iris, hyacinth, gladioli, tulip and crocus. Some, like the *Narcissus serontinus* and *Urginea maritima* (Sea Aquill or giant hyacinth) bloom with the onset of the autumn rains, while others flourish in the Maltese springtime. At this season the countryside is at its best for otherwise bare-looking hillsides come to life with rosemary, fennel, oregano, thyme, broom and heather, the latter an important source of nectar for Malta's honey bees and other insects.

FIELD AND CULTIVATED FLOWERS

Springtime is when most of Malta's fruit trees are in blossom, their delicate hues taming the riot of colour seen in the hedgerows and fields. From March onwards is the season of the rosy-purple sulla (*Trifolium purpureum*), the giant clover grown as a fodder crop. Other colourful carpets that flourish for a time in fallow lands, meadows and waste areas are a variety of daisies, cowslips and vivid displays of yellow and red poppies. If not in the field, then certainly in representation, visitors will come across the 'Malta Knap-weed', belonging to the genus *Centaurea*. This purplish thistle-like flower, supported by long stalks with narrow grey-green leaves, is the national plant of the islands.

Among the most common of the ornamental flowering shrubs is the summer-blooming oleander whose pink and white flowers are seen in parks, private gardens and along roadsides. Another decorative plant, often set in traffic islands, is the lantana with its spikes of yellow or orange flowers. Bougainvillea grows readily and its purple and bright red bracts (for it is these rather than their inconspic-uous flowers that provide the colour) twine over doors, gateways and along stone walls. Geranium displays in earthenware pots or painted cans are also ubiquitous. Many succulents and cacti thrive in Malta's driest areas, especially the agave and 'prickly pear' (*Opuntia*) which makes good hedgerows and bears its pink or yellow thorny fruit in

Flowers and plants on sale at a stall in Republic Street, Valletta

September. Malta has a flourishing Cactus and Succulent Society, founded in 1951 to promote the study and cultivation of these plants.

Fauna

Changes in vegetation cover and a shortage of water have restricted, in numbers and varieties, indigenous fauna. Hunters and trappers have also played a major part, the once large wild rabbit population being almost decimated. Species that survive today include hedgehogs, rats, mice and many different kinds of lizard, including a unique variety on Fifla which successfully survived the bombardments when this island was used as a gunnery and target practice for the RN and RAF. In addition there are four species of snake, though rarely are they seen. Three are harmless and the fourth is not deadly.

INSECTS

These are far more common and the islands have a large variety of beetles and about two dozen species of butterfly, though the rapid pace of development has progressively robbed the latter of many of their habitats. The wealth of spring flowers provides butterflies with abundant nectar and clouds of them can often be seen around favoured bushes where they compete with honey bees. Visitors will recognise the Red Admiral, Large White, Painted Lady and Swallowtail. Of the many moths the Humming-bird Hawk, hovering amidst flowers, is the most fascinating.

BIRDS

The small range of habitats also restricts the resident bird population, the most common species being sparrows, finches, warblers, larks, jackdaws and thrushes, including Malta's national bird, the blue rock thrush whose habitat is cliffs and other inaccessible places. Visitors should watch out for kestrels hovering against the wind as they search for small mammals. The barn owl, peregrine and quail have also been known to breed on the islands, but they are rare. The herring gull is the commonest type of sea bird and, along with others, breeds on the cliffs, especially on Fifla which has been declared a nature reserve and permission from the Education Department is needed to land here. It is also the breeding ground for the Mediterranean shearwater, an aquatic diving bird of the puffin family.

Malta's bird population is greatly swelled by migrant species, for it is one of the Mediterranean's busiest staging posts for innumerable southbound and northbound birds who arrive and depart each autumn and spring. To save energy they ride on the thermal uplifts along their land routes but these air currents do not exist over the sea. This forces the birds to take the shortest sea crossings, such as the Strait of Messina and the Malta Channel, using the islands the way nature intended – stepping-stones between Africa and Europe. Well over 300 species have been logged some wintering on the islands, others passing through, not least flights of doves, ducks and honey buzzards.

This exciting time for ornithologists and all lovers of nature is marred by what has to be regarded as Malta's greatest shame, the irresistible impulse to shoot anything that flies. It shares this indictment with Italy and other

European countries. The scale of this bird slaughter is revealed by the fact that volunteers in 1989 found the bodies of some 4,800 honey buzzards floating in the Strait of Messina alone. When walking on Malta visitors will encounter or at least hear the shots of hunters, especially at weekends and holidays. They will also see fields and lanes littered with cartridges and dead birds. Bird-shooting is conducted from stone or wooden hides around which are rock pillars with cages containing net-caught sparrows and finches which act as decoys. For obvious reasons the incensed walker is advised to proceed with great caution in such areas, the most practical response being written protests to the authorities. With Malta on the brink of EEC membership it is of major importance that the policies of the EC's Directive of Conservation of Wild Birds be adopted. There is much local criticism of this wanton slaughter which has led to some protection legislature including wildlife sanctuaries at Buskett, Fifla island, Comino and Luqa Airport – not the best place for rifles! Mellieħa Bay has also become a conservation area, observatory and breeding ground for birds.

✠ PREHISTORY

Malta is heir to one of the most advanced yet enigmatic prehistories of the Mediterranean world, and for those interested in archaeology the rich vestiges of its distant past constitute a good enough reason for touring the islands. Visitors will be confronted with rock tombs, ancient village sites, dolmens, cart tracks and, most impressive of all, massive temple complexes. The latter are considered to be among the world's oldest free-standing monuments preceding in age the Egyptian pyramids by many centuries and Stonehenge by several millenia. These temple remains are now largely confined to the resistant outcrops of the Upper and Lower Coralline Limestone, though it is suggested that more once existed, particularly in central Malta. These, built of Globerigina Limestone, failed to resist both the rigours of weathering and the long centuries of farming practice when their worked stones provided convenient quarries for rural and other building projects. Who these temple builders were remains a partial mystery.

Prehistoric Chronology

Though still to be clarified in detail, archaeologists subdivide Malta's prehistory into the three broad time spans of Early Neolithic, Copper Age or Temple Culture and Bronze

Cultural Periods

Period	Type Site	Approx. Date
EARLY NEOLITHIC	Għar–Dalam Grey Skorba Red Skorba	5000–3750 BC
COPPER AGE/ TEMPLE CULTURE	Żebbug Mġarr Ġgantija Saflieni Tarxien	3750–2200 BC
BRONZE AGE	Tarxien Graves Borġ in-Nadur Baħrija	2200–900 BC

Age. These periods are further classified into cultural phases taking their names from 'type-site' discoveries which indicate development and change from one phase to the next. Some of these subdivisions, Żebbug for example, are recognised by pottery wares rather than monumental remains, which means that there is very little to see in the field. Such artefacts are displayed in the National Museum of Archaeology in Valletta (see page 104).

EARLY NEOLITHIC

The first traces of human occupation date to around 5000 BC when Neolithic (New Stone Age) settlers crossed the Malta Channel from Sicily. They brought a knowledge of sophisticated stone implements, agriculture (both pastoralism and cultivation), various crafts (including pottery) and the rudiments of an organised farming lifestyle. As noted (page 51) the islands were then well wooded and clearance for farming purposes began the irreversible process of deforestation. The crops they grew, initially under a basic system of shifting cultivation, included barley, wheat, leguminous plants such as lentils and madder, whose fleshy root provided a dark reddish–purple dye. As efficiency improved, sedentary farming developed and more land was increasingly cleared to support the needs of an expanding population. These early farmers had domesticated cattle, pigs, sheep and goats, with additional sources of food provided by hunting and the sea.

Some of the earliest evidence of this Neolithic economy comes from stratified deposits in Malta's many rock fissures and natural caves of which the type site is Għar-Dalam (see below). However, these early farmers probably lived in small settlements of wattle and daub huts, building materials unable to resist the erosion of time. More durable were their simple (at first) stone built shrines associated with fertility rites and mother goddess cults. The remains at Skorba (see below) mark the transition from the Early Neolithic to the Temple Culture proper.

THE TEMPLE CULTURE

It is uncertain whether the cultural advances of the Temple Period were local innovations or the result of new waves of colonists. The term Copper Age, equating Malta with the same time period developments in Sicily and Italy, is misleading, for no objects in this metal have been discovered at Maltese sites. The fact that stone technology continued throughout the Temple Culture suggests that the massive megalithic structures were indigenous developments on the islands.

Divided into five phases (see table), temple architecture evolved in sophistication from what were originally simple rock-cut tombs (e.g. Żebbug). From this blueprint a cloverleaf arrangement of chambers emerged (Mġarr) which rapidly developed into more complicated plans of two or three elliptical chambers set one behind the other and connected with the main entrance by passageways. This phase is represented by Ġgantija (see page 155) on Gozo and Tarxien (see below) on the main island, their plans representing the evolution in temple design and a hierarchy of religious sanctuaries.

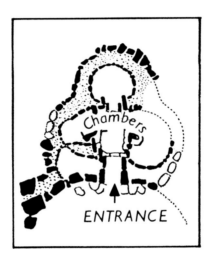

Basic structure of a Maltese temple

The temples were once roofed and each complex covered with stones and turf, for they were meant to be appreciated as interior ritualistic progressions. Now open to the sky the structures of the chambers are fully revealed, the most impressive elements being the limestone monoliths, many tons in weight, which are accurately cut, positioned and joined to their neighbours. Such craftmanship was achieved with stone implements, ropes, rollers and rough pulleys, not to mention mammoth human effort, albeit spread over many generations. One major clue to their building, especially the conveyance of stones from quarries, is the mysterious cart tracks (see below) which appear to be remnants of some prehistoric transport system.

It appears that the large temple complexes were not

burial places but were dedicated to the worship of the life cycle and fertility cults. Their interiors were decorated in many ways and fitted with altar and oracular chambers. Fat female figures, the personification of fruitfulness, were sculptured from stone or modelled in clay, and examples of these steatopygic goddesses can be seen in the National Museum of Archaeology. The consensus view is that the temples were prototypes for the elaborate Hypogeum of Hal Saflieni whose purpose, however, was somewhat different (see below).

THE BRONZE AGE

The Temple Culture period seems to have ended abruptly. The sanctuaries were quickly abandoned, ironically at the height of their architectural and artistic development. There has been much speculation about this curious hiatus though it seems unlikely that the apparently peaceful and undefended inhabitants were the victims of warlike metal-armed invaders. More plausible explanations are epidemics, possibly plague, or prolonged drought and famine, the latter caused by water shortage and perhaps augmented by population pressure on available farming resources.

Culturally and economically poorer, the three phases which form the Bronze Age relate not to continuous development but to separate waves of colonisation, the first by peoples who might have arrived from the Taranto region of southern Italy. Transforming the Tarxien area into a huge crematoria they are known as the Cemetery Folk who also built dolmens (megalithic tombs) throughout the islands. Silician migrants followed and take the name Borġ in-Nadur from the site of one of their fortified settlements above Birżebbuġa. Around 900 BC a third incursion of Bronze Age peoples from Sicily or southern Italy are given the name Baħrija from the type-site village south of the bay of Fomm ir-Riħ on Malta's west coast. They appear to have co-existed and culturally blended with the earlier Bronze Age settlers.

By 1000 BC there is evidence of Phoenician influence on the islands and around 800 BC these powerful merchant–colonists from the eastern Mediterranean had established trading posts on Malta. This effectively brought Maltese prehistory to its close, and heralded the lengthy period when the development of these islands was fashioned by a continuous, but varied sequence of foreign rule.

Visiting the ruins

Those with private transport can easily plan their own

prehistoric and temple-visiting tours but, as noted, some of the type-sites mentioned in the chronological table are not necessarily the best preserved and monumental. The venues described below are listed (bearing in mind cultural overlap) in developmental sequence and can be visited in this order, but such an itinerary would involve considerable backtracking. All can be reached as part of the general tours described on pages 115 to 145 and are relatively accessible by bus, though reaching some of them entails walking from village or other termini.

Għar-Dalam

Geologically and culturally this site is of great significance for its fossil remains and human artefacts date back to earliest times. Its name means 'Cave of Darkness', though so much has it revealed of the beginnings of life on Malta that 'Cave of Light' seems a more appropriate title. Located to the north of Birżebbuġa this water-eroded cavern extends some 215 metres into the limestone slopes of Wied Dalam which reaches the coast at St George's Bay, one of the inner indentations of Marsaxlokk Bay.

Għar-Dalam was excavated in the latter half of the nineteenth century and its stratified deposits revealed the countless remains of numerous extinct fauna, including dwarf elephants and hippopotami, giant dormice and land tortoises, anserines (related to the goose family) and other bird genera. These inhabited the islands when Marsaxlokk Bay was probably a large freshwater lake, lending weight to the overland migration theory and Malta's former connection with continental land masses. However, this physical link appears to have been with Europe rather than Africa, for the faunal remains are more characteristic of European species. The large number of bones has been explained by Għar-Dalam acting as a swallow-hole trap for animals.

Though greatly disturbed by later occupants the cave's upper deposits revealed the detritus of Stone Age peoples – fragments of human skeletons, the bones of hunted animals and carbonised grains. But whether the cave was fully inhabited or merely acted as a refuge or a place of burial, remains unknown. Other than its impressive size and some limestone formations there is little to see today, though the small museum provides an informative display on this primeval period of Maltese development.

On the opposite side of Wied Dalam, and within easy walking distance, is Borġ in-Nadur but both the temple and Bronze Age village are poorly preserved. More intriguing are the limestone etched 'cart tracks' which lead directly to the sea.

Skorba

Those wishing to visit the temples and other remains in chronological sequence should head for Skorba, though the route from Birżebbuġa passes close to the temple complexes of Hagar Qim and Mnajdra (see below). The Skorba ruins lie to the west of the small village of Zebbiaħ, close to the road to Chajn Tuffieħa. Excavated in 1961–63 the site proved to be of major importance in temple evolution, the original trefoil patterns being substantially modified in the Tarxien phase. A major discovery was two superimposed prehistoric villages distinguished by their grey and red pottery wares. Here can also be seen the remnants of Malta's oldest wall (c. 3600 BC) which, with the remains of farmers' huts establishes Skorba as the island's earliest proven settlement.

Less than a kilometre's walk to the west, on the outskirts of Mġarr are the Ta' Hagrat temples with similar though later remains. The pottery belongs to what is known as the Mġarr phase.

Haġar Qim and Mnajdra

These two complexes belong to the great period of temple building and both can be reached from the village of Qrendi. The nearest, Haġar Qim ('Standing Stones') involves a 20-minute walk south-westwards from the village, the sign-posted road skirting the inner part of Wied Hoxt above which, and visible from afar, is the temple's restored monumental façade. This structure is now unique, for it is built entirely of Globerigina Limestone, its pitted megaliths indicating centuries of weathering and erosion. Near the northeast wall, one of these stones (7m by 3m) rivals another massive block at Ġgantija as the largest quarried stone in the islands.

Haġar Qim also differs from other temples in the arrangement of its chambers which appear to have been added to the original plan without any attempt to preserve the basic trefoil arrangement. Other interesting details include complicated stone-cut decorations, the oracular chamber and 'mushroom' and 'table' altars. Many of Malta's fat divinities were once housed at Haġar Qim, including one of the most famous – a squat, skirted cult figure with piano legs and now headless. This 'Venus of Malta' is displayed in the National Archaeological Museum.

Less than half-a-kilometre downhill from Haġar Qim is the twin-temple complex of Mnajdra whose setting, even closer to the sea, makes it one of the most beautiful and evocative of Maltese ancient monuments. Though contemporary with Ħaġar Qim it is better preserved for it is less exposed to the elements and has outer walls of Coralline Limestone. Here too are rich stone decorations and the lower temple, probably the older, has a monumental stepped entrance.

The Hypogeum

Whereas surface temple complexes are common to the islands, Malta has only one *hypogeum*, the Greek word for an underground temple sanctuary used for burials. Its name, Hal Saflieni, is taken from the street in Paola where, in 1902, workers building houses and digging drains discovered it by accident. Professionally explored by Themistocles Zammit, it is one of Malta's most fascinating prehistoric sites and, together with the nearby Tarxien temple ruins, provides a fitting climax to a tour – though for some it will be the start – of Maltese ancient monuments.

The Hypogeum is a fantastic labyrinthine complex of subterranean burial and temple chambers hollowed into the local rock and arranged on three levels. The uppermost, by which the complex is entered, is the oldest and was probably a natural cave system, its burial chambers being the roughest cut. Here descent is made by a modern spiral staircase into the darker and gloomier levels, the bane of claustrophobics and sufferers of vertigo. The main chamber of the middle level is one of expertly curved and corbelled walls (more than reminiscent of the architectural features of the above-ground temples) which are punctuated by expertly carved niches and doorways leading to side chambers, some still retaining evidence of painted decorations. One such chamber is the so-called 'Holy of Holies' and another, the Oracle Chamber, has an eerie echo effect. In the main chamber was found the cult figure of the 'sleeping lady', now in the National Archaeological Museum. The Hypogeum's lowest level, 14 metres below street level and reached by a sinisterly narrow and uneven staircase, leads to more pits, graves and tombs.

When the Hypogeum was first explored some 7000 inhumations with their grave goods were discovered and scholars trace the prototypes of this sophisticated cemetery to the rock burial chambers of the Żebbuġ and Mġarr phases, the Xemxija tombs on the north side of St Paul's Bay belonging to the latter. But the theory is that the Hypogeum was not only a burial place but also a prestigious sanctuary for the training of priests and priestesses in oracular and other cults. A number of artefacts support this hypothesis.

Tarxien

From the Hypogeum it is a short walk through the grid-planned streets of Paola to the temple ruins of Tarxien which are to the north of the old agricultural village of the same name. They were also discovered by chance, in this

TARXIEN

BOUNDARY WALL

FIRST

TEMPLE

SECOND

hearth

TEMPLE

Entrance

Entrance

THIRD TEMPLE

MAIN
ENTRANCE

case by a local farmer whose plough encountered great difficulty in negotiating the monoliths that were progressively uncovered in his fields. Themistocles Zammit again responded to the challenge of this new Maltese discovery and systematically excavated the complex between 1914 and 1919.

He uncovered three interlinked temple complexes, the latest one coinciding with the great period of temple building. This is reached from the main entrance beyond the museum which contains replicas of carved stones and other voluptuous goddesses. Amidst its complicated structures are other relief carvings of spirals and animals that played vital roles in the Stone Age economy – sheep, cattle, pigs and goats. The second temple consists of three double-lobed chambers of decreasing size, the circular hearth in the larger, outer chamber probably having been a cremation altar. Other animal carvings include bulls and a sow suckling her litter. The heavy stone balls under part of the lifted floor were the efficient rollers used to move the great stones. The first and oldest temple lies to the right of the second, beyond which are a number of round hollows used either for divining purposes or libation ceremonies. Another theory is their use for some sort of game. The Tarxien museum and Maltese bookshops have detailed guides to the site's remains. Many of its important relics have been removed to the Archaeological Museum in Valletta.

Cart Tracks

Ingrained in the stony limestone exposures of Malta and Gozo are criss-crossed patterns of parallel ruts of various widths. Though known as cart tracks they are not the fossilised products of ancient wheeled-transport but probably the result of simpler forms of conveyance such as slide carts. The theory is that these consisted of two wooden shafts attached to a draught animal (possibly an ox), the framework stabilised by wooden crossbars capable of supporting heavy loads of building materials, agricultural produce or even passengers. The ends of the main shafts might have been shod, and the weight of the load would impress itself into the then-existing soil cover and, in time, the soft underlying Coralline Limestone which, as noted, only becomes hard and resistant on exposure (e.g. when the soil cover is eroded). Over-deepened ruts would have impeded easy dragging and this might explain the duplication of 'new' tracks seen in many areas. It has been suggested that a system of cart junctions and 'shunting yards' operated, the latter allowing two carts approaching from opposite directions on the same track to continue on their course.

These tracks, an intriguing ancient transport system, are recognisable in many parts of the islands, for example, at Borġ in-Nadur and San Pawl tat-Tarġa (north of Naxxar). They are associated with post-Temple Culture village sites and this distribution, together with the fact that tombs of Punic origin (see page 68) are cut into some of them, suggests that they belong to the Bronze Age. Why many of these tracks terminate at high cliff edges remains, as yet, a mystery, one suggestion being – fanciful to most – that this lends weight to the theory of Malta's physical links with other Mediterranean land areas at this time.

A BRIEF HISTORY

Phoenicians and Greeks

Malta's recorded history begins somewhere around 1000 BC when Phoenicians from the eastern shores of the Mediterranean roamed the inland sea in their powerful naval and merchant vessels. With the protective eyes of Osiris on their bows they searched out trading bases that challenged the territorial expansion of the Greeks and, subsequently, the Romans. The Phoenicians were important middlemen through whose hands passed the trading and cultural influences between Mesopotamia and the Mediterranean, and to facilitate such international exchanges they are credited with the introduction of the alphabet. The unique Maltese language (see page 82) is regarded as originating as a Phoenician dialect which, with the passage of time, became adulterated by other colonising tongues.

The major Phoenician power in the western Mediterranean was Carthage whose ruins lie north of modern Tunis. Its political suzerainty extended over the colonies on Malta the first being sited close to the large anchorage of Marsaxlokk Bay. The area around Tas Silġ church, at the approach to the Delimara peninsula (see page 117), has revealed the remains of a temple dedicated to the deities Melqart (identified with the Greek Heracles) and Asarte (the Greek goddess Hera). Excavations in 1963–72 indicated that this was also the site of a prehistoric temple and a later Christian church, but the most important artefacts were discovered in 1691 – a pair of marble *cippi* (low pedestals for funerary dedications) which carried bilingual epigraphs in Phoenician and Greek. Together with linguistic evidence from other parts of the Mediterranean, they provided a major key to Phoenician decipherment and established its script as being the parent of European alphabets. One *cippus* can be seen in Malta's Archaeological Museum, its twin in the Louvre being a gift to Louis XVI of France by Grand Master Emmanuel de Rohan Polduc.

The Carthaginians were the first to recognise the defensive hill locations that became the sites of Mdina and Rabat (Victoria), the Maltese and Gozitan capitals. But their main interests were coastal and another trading and naval base was founded on the Grand Harbour as a means of consolidating Carthaginian positions on Sicily. Temple and other ruins have been discovered on the Corradino (Kordon) Heights, though the site of this port was probably at Birgu (Vittoriosa).

The Greeks visited Malta from the seventh century onwards, but there is no firm evidence of any formal colonisation. As noted, they called the place *Melita* which, like 'Malta' itself is probably a corruption of the Phoenician word *malat*, meaning 'port' or 'safe harbour', both Marsaxlokk Bay and the Grand Harbour providing such havens. Gozo or in Maltese Għawdex (pronounced OW-dehsh) is also said to be a Phoenician–Greek name derived from *gaulos* or *gaudos*, a type of small boat possibly similar to the *luzzu*, the traditional boats of the islands and now a Maltese trademark. The eyes of Osiris incorporated into their colourful decorations stresses such continuity.

Romans

The word *Punic* derives from the Latin *Poenus* and *Punicus* by which the Romans referred to the Phoenicians and Carthaginians. Punic is best known as the name given to the three wars in the third and second centuries BC when Rome and Carthage were embroiled in deadly struggle for mastery of the Mediterranean. Strategic Malta was inevitably a focal point in this protracted conflict and in the second Punic War (218–201 BC) the islanders, provoked by Carthage's excessive demands for money, resources and manpower, sided with Rome. This enabled the consul Tiberius Sempronius to take Malta in 218 BC, though Carthage was not conquered until 146 BC.

The Romans also referred to both Malta and its capital as Melita, and the latter was expanded and refortified to extend over much of the area now occupied by Rabat. Granted a measure of autonomy, Malta initially prospered under Rome but this was abruptly terminated when the administration of the islands passed to the province of Sicily. Gaius Verres, governor from 73–70 BC, pillaged Malta of its natural resources and temple treasures, leaving the islands vulnerable to hordes of rapine pirates. The Maltese point out that similar spoliation was repeated some nineteen centuries later at the hands of Napoleon Bonaparte, the riches of the Baroque churches then being the prize of conquest.

Verres systematically ruined what had been one of Rome's richest dominions, but conditions gradually improved with the empire's reorganisation under Augustus. Malta was administered by a procurator whose official title was 'the first' – *protos* in Greek and *primus* in Latin. Though these were the administrative languages the day-to-day culture of the islanders appears to have remained Punic. *Acts* 28, detailing the apostle Paul's association with Malta, refers to the locals as 'barbarians', the original sense of this word meaning those unable to speak the classical languages. Yet it has been suggested that the Phoenician dialect they spoke might have been similar enough to Aramaic for Paul to understand and converse with them. Like Phoenician, Aramaic was a Semitic language and an important *lingua franca* throughout the Levant and parts of the Mediterranean.

ST PAUL AND CHRISTIANITY

The outstanding event in Malta's Roman history is the apparent conversion of the islanders to Christianity by Paul. Journeying from Caesarea in Palestine to stand trial in Rome, the heavy winter seas and shipwreck which brought him and his companions to Malta (probably in 60 AD) is graphically related in *Acts*. According to the Roman scholar Pliny the Elder, few ships sailed in central Mediterranean waters between November and February and Paul's party was forced to stay on Malta for three months before the centurian in charge was able to organise a safe passage to Syracuse in Sicily.

Hospitably received by the Roman *primus*, Publius, Paul lost no time in preaching the Christian message and healing the sick, including Publius's father who was suffering from acute bouts of fever and dysentery. There were other 'miracles', including the famous story of Paul being bitten by a viper yet, to the acclaim of the islanders, suffering no ill effects. Throughout Malta the saint is usually depicted in the act of shaking the snake from his hand, thus ridding the islands of deadly serpents (see page 55).

According to tradition Publius was converted to Christianity and became Malta's first bishop only, like many of the islanders, to suffer Roman persecution and martyrdom. Despite this and the spread of Islam in subsequent centuries, the islanders remained loyal to the Christian faith they still deeply cherish. Their indebtedness to St Paul is everywhere apparent and it is impossible to escape from the influence he still holds over Malta. Seeking out the sites associated with the apostle forms the basis of an absorbing island excursion.

Byzantines and Arabs

With the collapse of the Roman West, Malta passed to the

rule of the Eastern Roman or Byzantine Empire whose capital was Constantinople. This marked an indistinct period in the history of the islands, though they acted as a strategic base for Constantinople's reconquest of North Africa from the Vandals and were visited by Belisarius, the brilliant general of the Byzantine Emperor Justinian. There is evidence that the capital, Melita, continued as an important trading centre and the countryside around retained agricultural villas (some excavated) which produced grains, olives and vines.

In AD 870 the Byzantine garrison fell to the Aghlabid Caliphs, Arab rulers who already controlled much of Spain and the southern parts of France, Italy and Sicily. From Melita (which they called Medina) and a fortress (the forerunner of San Angelo) at Birgu, they tolerantly ruled Malta until 1090. There is little evidence of religious persecution and many Maltese willingly joined the Arab forces to defend the islands against Byzantine reprisals. Unlike Moorish Spain Malta has no legacy of mosques and alcazars (palace-fortresses), though certain architectural styles are the products of this formative period, not least the shuttered wooden balconies that characterise homes throughout the islands. Originally a *purdah* device for the seclusion of women, they still offer the housewife and others a private vantage point for viewing street activities.

Perhaps the main landscape influence of the Arabs was that which changed the Maltese countryside. These rulers were a highly cultured people whose science and technology were far in advance of anything Europe could offer at the time. They introduced many efficient farming techniques

Wrought iron balconies are also features of Maltese domestic architecture

(especially irrigation) already tested elsewhere, and the cultivation of cotton, citrus fruits and other crops led to such descriptions of the islands as being 'rich in everything that is good'. Many Arab farming and land use terms entered the Maltese language and a large proportion of place names date from this period. In fact, the greatest impact of the Arabs was the modifications they introduced into the kindred Maltese language (see page 82) which may have remained essentially Phoenician up to this point.

A Medieval Pawn

Divided by quarrelling factions the Arabs were unable to resist the advances of the Normans who had already secured much of southern Italy and Sicily. Count Roger, a member of the prestigious Hauteville family, landed in Malta in 1090 and quickly established the islands as a defensive outlier of Sicily. According to tradition he tore off part of his red personal standard and gave it to the islanders as an emblem. To this they added a white section thus achieving, with the later inclusion of the George Cross insignia (see page 78), the country's present flag. Though tolerant of Islam, Roger established Malta as a Christian stronghold and the Norman grip tightened under Roger II (1095–1154) who firmly welded Malta, Sicily and southern Italy into a single kingdom.

For some centuries the same fate and vicissitudes as befell the Sicilians were shared by the Maltese. When Constance of Sicily married Henry VI of Hohenstaufen the islands came under Swabian (1194) influence, only to pass to the Angevins (1266), the Aragonese (1284) and the Castilians (1412), all leaving their palaces to stand in the old city of Medina (Mdina). Often granted as fiefs to extortionate noblemen the islands suffered heavy taxtion and general neglect which left them at the mercy of Saracen and other raiding parties. Discontent led to a number of rebellions and in 1428 a limited self-governing administration – the *Università* – forged a closer relationship with Castille, Alfonso V controlling the islands directly without the aid of greedy landlords. From Mdina the *Università* effectively governed Malta until 1530 when the islands were granted as a permanent home to the Knights of St John by Charles V, son of Philip I of Castile. Taking the title of Holy Roman Emperor (1519–58), Charles V became the greatest Habsburg and the most powerful ruler in Europe. His ceding of Malta to the Knights forged much of the subsequent destiny of the islands.

The Knights of St John

The origin of the Knights long precedes their acquisition of Malta. In 1070 some Italian merchants from Amalfi founded the hospice of St John the Almoner, near the Church of the Holy Sepulchre in Jerusalem. It was manned by a brotherhood of 'hospitallers', then a religious order dedicated to caring for the sick and weary who had made the long pilgrimage from Europe to the Christian shrines of the Holy Land. Following the capture of Jerusalem by the Crusaders in 1099, many gifts of European money and fiefs of land were granted to the hospitallers and a Papal Bull of 1130 conferred upon them the rights to take up arms in defence of themselves, their hospice and Jerusalem against Moslem and other threats. Their transformation into a military body was swift and massive castles were built throughout Palestine, only to fall in time to the Saracens, the name the West gave to the Moslem adversary.

When Acre, the last Christian fortress, was captured the hospitallers – now known as 'the Knights' – briefly settled on Cyprus before making Rhodes their powerful headquarters from 1310 to 1523. Together with their control of other Dodecanese islands and many strategic points on the Asia Minor mainland, the Knights of Rhodes successfully challenged the westward tide of Islam, their major foes by the fifteenth century being the Ottoman Turks. Though withstanding a number of Ottoman sieges, ultimately they were unable to resist the massive forces of Suleiman the Magnificent, the greatest of the Ottoman sultans (1520–66). It took six months before the Knights were forced to surrender, and to honour their heroism Suleiman allowed them to leave Rhodes with their arms, ships and moveable property.

Led by the proud and valiant Philip Villiers de l'Isle-Adam, last of the Rhodian Grand Masters (1521–22), the Knights temporarily moved to Viterbo and Civitavecchio before accepting Charles V's offer of Malta. In the late autumn of 1530 the Order's galleys dropped anchor off Birgu in what is now Dockland Creek. They were accompanied by several thousand Rhodians which explains the common Maltese surname *Crech* (Greek).

MALTA UNDER THE KNIGHTS

The Knights had been sceptical of basing themselves on Malta, but they had nowhere else to go. The worrying clause in Charles V's agreement was the insistence that they also defended Tripoli (then under Spanish control), the expectation being that the military manning of this strategic sea channel would deter Ottoman galleys from entering the western Mediterranean basin. Neither were the islanders pleased, for they viewed the arrival of the Knights as a breach of their privileges formerly recognised by the *Università*. Though l'Isle-Adam promised to respect the Maltese administration, much of it had been eroded before his death in 1534 and subsequent Grand Masters (see page 161) strengthened their bureaucratic control. The Knights were under no illusion that Malta, christened the 'new stronghold of the hellhounds' by the Ottomans, would remain unchallenged for long and they co-opted local labour into repairing old fortifications and building new. Continuing to reside in Mdina, the landed nobles had little influence on what was happening in the area of the Grand and Marsamxett Harbours which the Knights saw as both offensive and defensive keys to survival. They protected these with promontory forts and other defences, not least the magnificent St Elmo fortress which, along with its acolytes, guarded the entrances to both waterways.

Granted a respite of some fifteen years before again being militarily challenged, the Knights quickly re-established the hierarchical order which had governed their organisation on Rhodes. They continued to recruit from the noble Catholic houses of Europe and following a successful probationary period the 'novice' Knight was allowed to take the vows of chastity, poverty and obedience to which was added the solemn promise never to take up arms against a Christian. Waging war on the 'infidel' Moslem was a different matter and further vows included those of never to surrender or show cowardice as 'Soldiers of the Cross'. Only then could a novice become a Knight and don the Order's black mantle with its eight-pointed linen cross resting over the heart.

At the head of the Order was the Grand Master, elected by the senior Knights and nominally subject to the decisions of the Council or Chapter General. Nineteen Grand Masters had served on Rhodes and a further 28 (see page 161) ruled on Malta their power (though technically subject to the Pope) being, in effect, absolute. As on Rhodes the Knights were divided into nationalities or *langues*, these original 'tongues' being France, Provence, Auvergne, Aragon, Castile and Leon, Portugal, Italy, Germany and England. Each *langue* was headed by a *pilier* (prior) and collectively lived in an *auberge* (inn or hostel), usually located close to the ramparts and other defences they were required to defend and maintain.

The Order also supported and relied on 'lesser' members

(those not of noble birth) which included Sergeants of Arms (both soldiers and nurses), Chaplains (hospital and church overseers) and administrators for the hundreds of *command-eries* scattered across Europe, many of them royal gifts in appreciation of the Order's valiant stand against Islam. The Knights relied on the money that came from these estates, though the conventual treasury was further replenished by the spoils from their mercenary activities on Ottoman shipping. Despite their vows, the Maltese Knights were anything but poor and neither could they be called pious celibates. As the years progressed the problems of dissolute ways and lax discipline were compounded by internal dissension and many have argued that this was the result of conceit and self-aggrandisement that followed the most remarkable campaign in the Order's history – the defeat of the Turks in 1565.

THE GREAT SIEGE

The Knights continued to be a thorn in the side of the territorial ambitions of the Ottomans who, in 1551, sacked Gozo and made slaves of thousands of its islanders. The mighty Sultan Suleiman, now past his seventieth year, reserved his major attack on Malta for 1565, affording the Knights extra time to complete their defences, especially of the St Elmo and St Angelo fortresses. Aware of the gravity of the situation, Grand Master Jean Parisot de la Vallette's plea for European assistance was ignored and when the siege came only 600 Knights and some 9000 enlisted troops stood alone against 81 Ottoman ships conveying an army in excess of 30,000. With the fall of St Elmo after 31 days of merciless siege the Turks had already lost thousands of men, including one of their champions, Dragut, whose name the Maltese commemorate in Dragut Point at the entrance to Marsamxett Harbour. To prevent Ottoman galleys from entering what is now Dockland Creek and Birgu – the Knights' headquarters – chains and other obstacles were hastily erected. The Turks pounded all positions, but the Knights retaliated with even more precision. The heat and disease took a savage toll on both armies, but it was the Turks who suffered the gravest casualties with some two-thirds of their attacking force killed. Exhausted and demor-alised their retreat was inevitable and this was further prompted by the news that the Sicilian Viceroy, Garcia de Toledo had despatched reinforcements to aid Malta. They were not needed for the Turks sailed away in September and with their defeat at Lepanto, some six years later, much of the Mediterranean was restored to being a Christian sea.

Birth of a City

The magnificent fortress-city of Valletta, purposely built for defence, was a consequence of the Great Siege and the inspiration of de la Vallette who vowed that the Knights would retreat no further than Malta. With the backing of Pope Pius IV and financial support from a grateful Europe, work quickly began on a planned city whose virgin site was the rocky, ridge-like peninsula of Sceberras, bounded by the Grand and Marsamxett Harbours and their subsidiary creeks. On 28 March 1566, de la Vallette ceremoniously laid the first stone of the city that has since borne his name.

Valletta's design, including its fortifications, was the inspired work of the Italian Francesco Laparelli, a foremost exponent of military architecture in sixteenth-century Europe. The plan called for the levelling of the peninsula and considerable work was undertaken, but finance and an expected return of the Turks dictated that more urgent defensive work took precedence. The street pattern followed the original plan of a rectangular grid and the main thoroughfares paralleled the central Strada Reale, now Republic Street, which continues to follow the peninsula's length for 1.5 kilometres from City Gate to St Elmo Fort, the latter repaired and strengthened by Laparelli. Regularly intersecting these access ways were the cross-streets which dropped down to the fortified shores. These, the 'cursed streets of stairs' of which Byron doggedly complained, retain their steepness or stepped character.

Dying in 1568 at the ripe old age of 72, la Vallette failed to see his dream completed, and the building of Valletta was energetically continued by Grand Master Pietro del Monte

Landscaped gardens are features of Valletta's battlements above the Grand Harbour

San Savino (1568–1572). By this time Laparelli's work had been taken over by the Maltese civil engineer, Girolamo Cassar and much of Valletta today is essentially his work. Del Monte organised the Order's move from Birgu to Valletta and Cassar was responsible for most of the city's public buildings – the Palace of the Grand Masters, the co-cathedral of St John (which he shared with Laparelli), most of the auberges and many parish churches and convents. His son, Vittorio was also responsible for the architectural embellishment of Valletta, as were other local and foreign builders.

But the obsession continued to be with fortifications and another new city, a landward extension of Valletta, was inaugurated in 1724. Taking the name Floriana – from the earlier plans of the Italian engineer Paolo Floriani – it was designed to strengthen the defences from the Grand Harbour to Pietà Creek. Not surprisingly, the Turks never returned to Malta and the Knights safely prospered within their defences of curtain walls, moats, bastions, cavaliers and ravelins. However, by the eighteenth century trading emphasis had shifted away from the Mediterranean and corruption and decline had reduced the military might of the Turks. The Order's role became increasingly anachronistic and the French Revolution robbed it of considerable financial holdings. With discipline lax and growing disaffection amongst the islanders, the Order's reaction to Malta's next invasion was anything but courageous.

Enter the French

Recognising the strategic worth of Malta to his imperialistic ambitions, Napoleon Bonaparte sailed into Marsamxett Harbour in 1798 and Grand Master Ferdinand von Hompesch immediately surrendered, agreeing also to the Order's withdrawal from Malta. This was a swift evacuation and when Napoleon left for his campaigns in Egypt the French began their systematic looting of Malta's treasures. The islanders retaliated and with help from the King of Sicily and Nelson's blockade of the central Mediterranean, the French surrendered in 1800. Though formally restored to the Order (Treaty of Amiens, 1802), Malta was temporarily administered by Captain Alexander Ball whose clever political tactics paved the way for Britain's takeover. In 1814, the Treaty of Paris officially ceded the islands to the British Crown for a period which lasted until 1964.

Under the Union Jack

Approaching the height of its own imperialistic power,

Britain developed Malta as a major naval base and communications centre. It became the headquarters of the British Mediterranean Fleet and an important coaling station, especially after the opening of the Suez Canal in 1869. The dockyard rapidly expanded to employ thousands of Maltese and the countryside prospered as improved methods and irrigation fostered such crop specialisation as potatoes, cotton and vines. The role of the Grand Masters was now replaced by that of the British Governors, a total of thirty-four serving Malta from 1814 to 1964. Though Britain did much to develop the infrastructure of the islands, more especially on Malta itself, there were periods of disquiet and moves for greater autonomy. The local riots of 1919 led to the introduction of internal self-government but Britain, through its governors, retained control in imperial matters and foreign affairs.

Dissident voices against British rule continued, but the main threat to Malta was now the fascist ambitions of Mussolini and his allies. Internal friction was set aside as rulers and islanders waited the inevitable, the islands becoming the embattled Mediterranean fortress of World War II. Known as the Second Great Siege, this period of shared courage and endurance forged the closest bonds between British and Maltese.

THE SECOND GREAT SIEGE

There are many islanders who proudly remember Malta's 'finest hour', some fifty years ago. The stories are epic and begin with the Gladiator bi-planes, *Faith, Hope* and *Charity*, the RAF's sole fighting force when Italy entered the war on Germany's side in 1940. For three weeks they challenged the enemy attack and the only survivor was *Faith*! Another major feat was the towing into the Grand Harbour of the awashed tanker *Ohio* which contained enough salvaged fuel to avert total surrender. All anti-aircraft defences had rationed ammunition and the routes taken by their supply convoys became bomb alleys. With the arrival of air and naval (including submarine) reinforcements, Malta was able to block Axis manoeuvres in the central Mediterranean, and these were essential to supplying Rommel's campaigns in North Africa.

With many of the islanders forced to shelter in Valletta's and Floriana's stout defences, Malta's apocalypse came when some 3000 Italian and German bomber raids inflicted a massive death toll and destroyed in excess of 30,000 buildings. For its size the main island of Malta, but chiefly the Valletta conurbation, holds the dubious honour of being the most bombed area in the world. The destruction exacerbated the already prevalent problems of supply shortages, not least food, and disease. But torn and bereaved Malta survived this most crucial time in its history and gained a personal tribute from President Roosevelt. For the islanders, however, their proudest honour was the collective award of the British George Cross (see page 4) and the simple plaque in Valletta can easily be missed. Affixed to the outside wall of the former Palace of the Grand Masters (now the Maltese Parliament Building) it reads:

The Governor
Malta   Buckingham Palace

To honour her brave people I award the George Cross to the island Fortress of Malta to bear witness to a Heroism and Devotion that will long be famous.

April 15th, 1942   George R.I.

Independence

After the war the British financially assisted Malta's recovery and reconstruction, but the real question was the political future of the islands. Proposals for complete integration with the UK floundered and, instead, Malta became a self-governing country within the British Commonwealth. This was in 1964 and Independence Day is celebrated on 21 September. Under a defence agreement the British Forces were to remain for a period and further financial aid provided for the diversification of the Maltese economy, still heavily dependent on British military spending. On 13 December 1974, Malta was declared a republic and this annual date is also a national holiday. But the Union Jack was not finally lowered until 1 April 1979, when the British Forces finally pulled out. This occasion terminated several years of friction between the UK and the then Maltese Prime Minister, Dom Mintoff, who christened the withdrawal as Freedom Day (celebrated on 31 March). For many British and Maltese alike this official parting was a sad one and though the islanders are proud of their independence their bond with Britain remains strong. This is readily apparent in their fund of goodwill towards the thousands of British visitors to the islands and the many UK residents on Malta and Gozo.

Postscript

What of the Knights? The Order of St John still survives, its work having long reverted to its founding principles of medicine and caring for the sick. It has hospitals and clinics in many parts of the world and retains a headquarters in Valletta. In June 1968, His Most Eminent Highness Fra Angelo de Majana was the first Grand Master to return to Malta in state since the Order's eviction by Napoleon. However, the Order's continuity is best known through the voluntary work of the St John's Ambulance whose proud insignia is the eight-pointed Maltese Cross.

CULTURE AND ECONOMY

National Characteristics

It is impossible to characterise a people without resorting to over-generalisation. This is certainly a problem with the Maltese whose national traits and qualities have sometimes been dismissed as nothing more than the mixed product of the many peoples who have settled in these islands. There is more than an element of truth in this, but to suggest that the Maltese character is merely a *pot-pourri* of foreign elements is tantamount to insult.

Though the islands have played a traditional role as a cultural melting-pot (and continue to do so), the Maltese have a proud sense of national identity which long precedes their attainment of independence and republicanism. One of their main qualities is the ease with which they incorporate foreign ideas, but in a way that strengthens rather than erodes national consciousness and self-preservation. For many centuries both have been nourished by the two fundamental pivots of Maltese life – the unique language of the islanders and their singular attachment to the tenets of the Roman Catholic Church. For the Maltese, internationalism is a positive trait which has benefited their commercial zeal, not least today when tourism plays an increasingly major role in the economy. The genuine hospitality that once welcomed St Paul – the 'no small courtesy', as Luke wrote – continues to be shown to reciprocating visitors and there can be few parts of the world where the level of polite acceptance is so readily apparent.

The Maltese are an enterprising and hardworking people, but they also know how to enjoy life and have a well-developed sense of humour, many of their jokes directed at themselves. This point is more than proved in J S Arbela's *Malta and Gozo Explained* (available in island bookshops) which is an amusing compendium on all aspects of Maltese life. Himself a returned emigré it largely explains how the acceptance of foreigners has been further conditioned by the many Maltese who have emigrated in search of opportunity to most parts of the world, but mainly to the UK, USA, Canada and Australia.

Many would argue that the Gozitans are different to the Maltese, no less welcoming but more thrifty in character

Part of the individualism of the Maltese is displayed in their variety of door-knockers and letterboxes

and somewhat reserved. Its recent popularity with visitors has changed Gozo's parochial outlook, though gentle derision and badinage persists between the islands. On Malta the adjective *gbejniet* is levelled against the Gozitans, the suggestion being that their popular farm-made cheese (see page 39) should feature on the smaller island's coat-of-arms. The Gozitans reply that it is a more fitting Maltese emblem since most of it is exported to and consumed on the main island.

Language

The islanders are justly proud of their *Maltese* (or *Malti*), the spoken and written language that traces their cultural identity to ancient times. Probably beginning as a Punic dialect, its grammar and vocabulary came under strong Arabic influence, this composite Semitic tongue later acquiring Romance overtones (Norman–Sicilian, Italian and Spanish) prior to the onslaught of English. For centuries Maltese was a spoken language only, and chiefly one of the countryside. The spoken and written communication of medieval government, commerce and the church was Italian, though a number of Grand Masters are recorded as being proficient in Maltese.

It was the autocratic Sir Thomas Maitland, Malta's first British Governor (1813–24), who declared that English should replace the role of Italian, but only in 1921 did it become an official tongue and universally taught in schools. The status of Maltese was the cause of many political incidents, not least its validity in courts of law. Its rise to prominence as a written language resulted from the efforts of politicians (British and Maltese), philologists and local authors determined to write in their own vernacular. Along with English, Maltese became an official language in 1934 and has since been elevated to the status of national language. Maltese novels, poetry and plays have made similar literary strides.

The language that came to be written down uses 29 modified Roman characters, 24 being consonants and the remainder vowels:

a b ċ d e f ġ g għ h ħ i j k l m n o p q r s t u v w x z ż

Fourteen of the consonants have similar (but not identical) sounds in English, the remaining ten taking the following pronunciation: ċ (as in *ch*urch); ġ (*G*eorge); għ (as in *ah*r); ħ (as in the semi-glottal stop *ugh*); j (*y*et); q (not sounded when followed by a vowel, but at the end of a word or before a consonant pronounced as *k*); s (always a sibilant, hissing, sound as in *s*ea); x (*sh*op); z (*ts* as in ma*ts*); and ż (*z*inc). Maltese vowels – a, e, i, o, u – generally have pure sounds, one major exception being the *ie* diphthong, as in Tarxien (TAHR-sheen) and Sliema (SLEE(R)-mah).

Most visitors will be happy to discover that almost all the islanders speak fluent English and many have Italian as a

Some of Malta's country houses, like this one at St George's Bay, have been turned into hotels and leisure complexes.

third language. But for asking directions, or boarding buses and taxis, some mastery of Maltese pronunciation is needed. Though island names appear as fiercesome jaw-crackers the locals warm to those who attempt an approximation. The following contain most of the sound combinations found in Maltese place names: Birżebbuġa (beer-zeeb-BOO-jah); Siġġiewi (sij-JEE(R)-wee); Xagħra (SHAH-rah); Ħaġar Qim (haj-jahr-EEM); Marsamxett (mahr-sahm-SHEHTT); Xewkija (SHOO-kee-yah); Ġgantija (J'GAHN-tee-yah); Għar Dalam (ahr-DAH-lam) and Mġarr (im-JAHRR). In the latter the *m* is pronounced as *im* when followed by a consonant, as in Mdina (im-DEE-nah).

The influence of the Romance languages on *Maltese* makes some of the basic pleasantries easy to remember, and few will be lost to the meanings of *bonġu* (bon-JOO), *bonswa* (bon-SWAH), *skużi* (SKOO-zee) and *grazzi* (GRAHT-see). But, as if to flaunt its linguistic separateness, the Maltese for 'please' is *jekk jogħġbok* (yehkk YOJ-bok), and a most useful word is *sahha* (SAH-hah) which is a greeting, a goodbye and the equivalent of 'good health' or 'cheers'.

The Church

The Roman Catholic Church holds a special place in Maltese life, a recent survey indicating that 87 per cent of the population regularly attended mass. Catholicism, however, is more than a matter of churchgoing; it is a powerful conviction that influences most social and, at times, economic and political matters. The church has been both protector and repository of much of Malta's traditions and folklore and in few parts of the Mediterranean will visitors be as conscious of religion's visual impact. Malta and Gozo are islands of churches and chapels and each of the parishes (64 on Malta and 14 on Gozo) has at least one massive domed and ornately façaded edifice which, both literally and metaphorically, is the focus of the village or local district.

The parish church is the pride of the community and many of those in the *casals* (the older village centres) are Baroque masterpieces associated with such seventeenth-century architects as Tommaso Dingli, Giovanni Barbara, Lorenzo Gafà and Dominico Cachia. Presiding over tortuous mazes of village streets and houses, these churches flaunt the prosperity of Malta under the Knights and their building was possible only under the cloak of protection provided by the forts and defences. Architectural tradition is strong and churches, crowned by massive domes, continue to be built in the classical-Baroque style. Without question, the old villages, whose twisting lanes are punctuated by simple Maltese chapels, are among the main tourist attractions of the islands. It is unfortunate that straight, wide traffic avenues have been driven through the centres of many of them. Hopefully the traditional quality of the Maltese village will be saved from further destruction.

In addition to the legion of churches and chapels, the importance of religion is further indicated by the numerous statues to the Virgin and saints in public squares and at most street corners. Many of the latter are of eighteenth-century date when their attendant oil lamps also provided modest street illumination at night. These wayside shrines are carefully tended by neighbourhoods as are other wall and house niches with Christian statues. Another distinctive feature of Maltese vernacular architecture are religious ceramic plaques on most private houses, the latter also carrying individual names as well as street numbers.

Festivals

Together with its national holidays (see page 28) Malta celebrates many festivals and folkloric events which are woven into the calendar of the Catholic Church. The origins of some are couched in the mists of time, the ancient traditions having been incorporated into Christian feasts. Carnival is a case in point, this celebration of the primeval 'Rites of Spring' now heralding, in Christian values, the approach of Lent and Easter.

Carnival
Timed according to the peripatetic dates for Easter carnival,

a major Maltese festival, is held sometime in February or March. The event was formally reinstituted shortly after the arrival of the Knights who also used it to celebrate their victory in the Great Siege, the traditional sword dance, the *parata*, evoking the Turkish defeat. In the eighteenth century the high point of carnival was the carriage procession of the Order's dignatories through the streets of Valletta. Today the parade is anything but pompous and consists of a defile of colourful floats, brass bands and costumed walkers, many in grotesque masks. It is the climax of months of preparation, the result of professional artists and numerous amateurs working towards three boisterous, fun-filled days and nights. Valletta's processions draw the biggest crowds but, not to be outdone, Gozo's carnival, centred on Victoria, is usually held a week earlier.

Easter
Compared to carnival much of the Holy Week celebrations are solemn. Parish churches put on poignant Last Supper displays and prepare their life-size statues (each depicting a stage in Christ's Passion) for the sombre Good Friday procession. These figures are carried by hooded, bare-footed *penitenti*, followed by others wielding heavy wooden crosses or dragging weighty chains and other encumberances. The brass and drum dirges of the accompanying bands contribute to this impressively cheerless pageant, the frequent discordant notes adding to the general atmosphere of anguish.

Inevitably, Easter Sunday celebrations are happier and the 'Risen Christ' is paraded through the streets, often at break-neck speed, to the accompaniment of church bells and more vibrant band repertoires. The rest of the day is spent with family and friends when Easter eggs are exchanged and also *frigolli*, a type of iced almond and lemon pastry cut into Easter shapes.

Christmas and New Year
Compared to Britain and some other European countries Christmas is less commercialised and essentially a family occasion. It is a time when many Maltese working abroad return home and during the Christmas and New Year period flights to Malta are at a premium. Christmas trees adorn windows, carol singers are in evidence and most homes have their crib. Larger ones built by schools and institutions are open to the public with donations going to charity. The midnight mass is well-attended and the highlight of Christmas Day is the family meal of turkey and pudding.

Another British-inspired tradition is the Christmas pantomime at Valletta's Manoel Theatre.

New Year is a family occasion though many Maltese now eat out in hotels and restaurants. These also provide special New Year meals and entertainment for visitors.

The Mnarja

Pronounced *Im-NAH-yah*, this is the popular name for the Feast of St Peter and St Paul held at Buskett, a wooded area near Mdina, on 29 June. The name derives from 'luminaria' (illuminations) which referred to the bastions of Mdina which were lit by torches and bonfires to mark the event. Traditionally a harvest celebration whose origin is obscure, it is now a major folk festival attended by many music and dance companies. Maltese wines and dishes are served from booths and stalls, especially fried rabbit and other speciali-

A country packman in traditional dress

ties that sustain both participants and visitors throughout the night and into the next day. This enjoyable occasion is brought to an end by the hilarious horse and donkey races, the animals ridden bare-back.

The Festi
Most of the rural and urban parishes of Malta and Gozo celebrate the feast day (*festa*) of their local patron saint, usually during the month of July. For the villagers especially they are busy and exciting occasions and there is much competition between the parishes to stage a good show. The illuminated churches are further decorated with damask hangings and flowers, and village streets are strewn with flags, banners and lamps. Celebrations last up to five days and apart from church services and religious processions there are many light-hearted events such as sports competitions, folk dancing, firework displays and brass band marches. Visitors will soon realise that the local band is an important Maltese institution which 'plays' an active part in all celebrations as well as entering prestigious competitions.

It is during *festa* occasions that the national costume of the Maltese women is likely to be seen. This is a full-length black or blue silk dress often with a richly embroidered bodice and attached to it is a large umbrella-style headdress known as the *faldetta* or *ghonella*. Malta's Folkloric Dance Group and the annual Folk Festival attempt to preserve old customs, including national costume but, as elsewhere, these have yielded to modern pressures. Folk evenings staged in the larger hotels are reasonably authentic and visitors will be introduced to the *Mattija*, a standard country dance.

The Maltese Economy

SERVICES

With the withdrawal of the British and their military spending, Malta was forced to re-shape its economy which had largely been based on services to the Royal Navy and other UK military interests. Service industries remain paramount but are now related to the foreign earnings of tourism and Malta's increasing importance as a central and accessible Mediterranean conference centre. In recent years some 700,000 tourists, over half of them British, have annually visited the islands and planners have recognised the future growth potential of this market by further attracting other foreign nationals, especially more Germans and Scandinavians. Major advances have also been made in the financial sector and many politicians and businessmen recognise the possibilities of Malta becoming an offshore centre for European and North African banking and investment. Such views are currently colouring Malta's interest in, and negotiations with the EEC for the arguments of those who support full membership are strongly challenged by others who see more advantages in Malta becoming the 'Channel Islands' of the Mediterranean or an insular 'mini-Switzerland'.

MANUFACTURING INDUSTRY

Realising the need for economic diversification, the Malta Development Corporation (an autonomous government body) is responsible for the promotion of local industry and the attraction of overseas investment. Manufacturing sectors that have recently prospered include processed foods and drink, chemicals, rubber and leather products and electrical components. The main island has a number of important industrial estates, including that of Marsa which is also a focal point in Malta's road network. Tourism has also fostered local manufacturing and many small-scale firms profitably specialise in the production of souvenir glass, ceramic and textile wares.

The development of the Birżebbuġa–Marsaxlokk Bay area (see pages 122) as a 'Freeport Malta' zone has suffered a number of setbacks, but there is still confidence that its completion and efficient management will prove to be a major manufacturing and services growth-point.

Less problematic have been the successes of Malta's traditional seafaring traditions and the British naval dockyard is now converted for commercial ship-building and repairs. The yards of the Grand Harbour creeks are among the busiest in the Mediterranean and major employers. Visitors are recommended to take one of the harbour cruises from Sliema's Strand waterfront to view the impressive dock facilities capable of accommodating some of the largest vessels afloat. Smaller island yards specialise in the building and refurbishment of pleasure craft and Malta, with its many new marinas, has become a major yachting mecca.

AGRICULTURE

Though changing to meet modern demands, Maltese agriculture is still firmly rooted in the traditions of the past. For centuries the hardworking and inventive farmers have perfected ways of extracting the utmost from their dry, stony countryside. Their intensive land use methods still

Stone-built, cubic-style farmsteads still characterise the Maltese countryside

appear primitive, yet they are effective in producing valuable harvests from small fields unsuited to most forms of agricultural mechanisation.

Fertile soil is a precious resource and the smallest of productive pockets are carefully tended, even narrow cliff ledges (the *redums*) that precipitously descend to the sea. Such land terracing is ubiquitous, as are the dry-stone walls that divide the small fields and miniscule plots, some no more than a few square metres in size. Acting as property boundaries, these walls are also safeguards against the erosion of soils on steep slopes. Such is its shortage that soil has been imported from Sicily, and Malta has its Red Soil Law whereby those erecting buildings are compelled to hand over the topsoil for its distribution amongst farmers.

A number of land use categories can be recognised in the Maltese countryside. The cultivated areas are divided into irrigated fields known as *saqwi* and dry-farmed lands – those dependant on rainfall – called *baghli*. In addition there is *xaghra* or waste which is further divided between *blat* (essentially bare limestone outcrops) and *moxa* (maquis-covered land used for the periodic grazing of sheep and goats). Over the last few decades, however, the numbers of these animals has substantially fallen, especially the environmentally damaging goat population which has declined from some 37,000 to a present estimate of 5,000. Where the possibility arises former areas of *xaghra* have been reclaimed and planted with olives and fig trees, but many areas have also reverted to the wild, their terraces re-colonised by *maquis*.

The *baghli* lands grow winter fodder crops such as sulla (see page 53) and cereals, though three-quarters of Malta's grain consumption is imported, especially wheat. Dry-farming is now becoming a marginal enterprise and most farmers increasingly concentrate their efforts on irrigated areas. There has been considerable investment in water storage tanks, pumps, pipelines and sprinklers and a variety of profitable vegetables are grown. Important exports include potatoes, onions and tomatoes and, more recently, cut flowers. Malta also specialises in citrus production (oranges and tangerines) and peaches, apricots, figs and vines grow well.

Visitors will be conscious of many farming improvements and a more scientific management of water and land resources. However, many scenes from the past persist including the animal-drawn plough working in fields and farmers tending their smallest plots with spades and hoes. Currently, the biggest threat to farming and the countryside in general is urban expansion which is most marked on the main island. Here the invading tentacles of the Valletta conurbation and other growth-points show no signs of abatement.

URBAN MALTA

In 1990 the total population of the islands was estimated as 360,000. In view of their small territorial extent this figure gives them one of the world's highest population densities. Local overcrowding is compounded by the unequal distribution of people between the islands, Malta accounting for some 330,000 with the remainder on Gozo, except for the few residents of Comino. The main island also ranks as one of the world's most urbanised areas for the Valletta conurbation (which includes Floriana, the Three Cities, Sliema, Hamrun and other physically linked centres) contains what approaches two-thirds of the country's population. Modern expansion stems from the rapid growth in servicing industries, especially tourism and the retirement home boom, but it also relates to the welfare policies of the government and the spate of large residential suburbs catering for young families. Continually rising living standards, reflected in the level of car ownership, has transformed Malta into a commuter island with a massive daily flow of people into and out of Valletta and its environs. Living in the expanding suburbs and working in the capital is now a major aspect of Maltese life and the countryside has rapidly become a dwindling resource. The planners are faced with the major dilemma of equating the need for expansion with the equally important task of environmental protection. Malta's diminutive size is unhelpful to this challenge.

SPORTS AND ACTIVITIES

Visitors seeking something more than sun and sea will never be short of things to do on Malta, for there is a wide range of activities to suit every taste, age and interest. The sports enthusiast will find facilities for most outdoor and indoor pursuits and the less physically-motivated can choose from a variety of events and entertainments. In addition to the main religious and secular celebrations (see pages 84–87) the NTO publishes a complete list of current attractions including exhibitions, rallies and tournaments, cultural festivals and folk, pop and classical concerts. The information that follows can only outline a selection of what is available.

Bathing and Swimming

In summer, coastal relaxation and sea-based activities naturally come first with most visitors and also the Maltese. However, compared with some other parts of the Mediterranean, it has to be said that the islands are not over-endowed with large sandy beaches so swimming pools and lidos are necessary features of the higher-starred hotels. The beaches that do exist become extremely crowded for they are easily accessible by public transport and many of them are the focal points for tourist development. On Malta most of the resort beaches, with hotels and restaurants at hand, are in the north and north-west of the island. Here the most popular strands are Golden, Għajn Tuffieħa and Ġnejna Bays (to the west of Mġarr); White Tower, Armier and Paradise Bays (on the Comino-facing side of the Marfa Ridge); and Il Għadira (the island's longest sandy stretch) at the head of Mellieħa Bay. Elsewhere smaller beaches (some pocket-size) are found at Pretty and St George's Bays (Birżebbuġa), and at Marsaskala and St George's Bay at St Julian's.

On Gozo, Xlendi and Marsalforn Bays have limited sandy beaches, but this island's biggest stretch of sand is at Ir-Ramla, popularly known as Calypso's Bay and surprisingly uncommercialised. To the east of it is the idyllically isolated beach of San Blas Bay. Comino has no sandy shores.

Not all these beaches are safe for novice swimmers and care should be taken at all times. Despite its apparent tidelessness the Mediterranean is often afflicted with

Modern hotels and apartment blocks, Tower Road, Sliema

dangerous currents and undertows which respond to land and sea temperature changes and prevailing winds. Special care is needed when swimming from Malta's many rocky headlands and shores, even at such popular venues as Sliema, St Julian's and St Paul's Bays. Some of the most attractive coastal areas are extremely isolated and help in times of difficulty is rarely at hand.

Water Sports

Rocky coasts, clear seas and a rich marine life make snorkelling a fascinating pursuit and this can be done with minimal instruction and modest outlay on equipment. Breathing masks and other accessories can be bought or rented at beach centres. Many of the larger bays have facilities (and equipment for hire) for windsurfing and water skiing and several hotels also provide water skiing lessons. A major annual event is the windsurfing race betweeen Malta and Sicily which attracts competitors from many countries. Sea conditions permitting, this takes place towards the end of May and information is available from 'Wishbone Windsurfing Promotions' (tel: 314956).

The main summer spectator sport is waterpolo, played in specially constructed sea pools. Many coastal towns fiercely compete to win the championship which is organised by the Amateur Swimming Association (tel: 223481). This also stages swimming competitions from July to August.

SAILING

With its long tradition of seafaring Malta has excellent

facilities for the sailing fraternity. The showpiece is the Yacht Marina in Lazzaretto Creek, an arm of Marsamxett Harbour between Ta'Xbiex and Manoel Island, and other berths extend into Msida Creek to the south. Some 350 boats, up to 50 metres in length, can be accommodated in these creeks and the administration of the marina is controlled from the Yachting Centre, Manoel Island Bridge, Gzira, which also houses the Customs and Immigration Authorities. The marina is equipped with all communications and supply facilities, including duty-free stores. On the opposite side of Manoel Island, facing Sliema Creek, is Manoel Island Yacht Yard which carries on the tradition of boat-building and repair dating back to the time of the Knights. It also functions as a winter storage area for up to 300 yachts and other craft. On Malta, further berths and facilities are available at Qawra, Mellieħa Bay and in Marsamxett Harbour itself.

Located on the eastern side of Manoel Island is the Valletta Yacht Club (tel: 333109) which was once the Royal Malta Yacht Club, founded in 1835. This prestigious fraternity has all details on the sailing regattas and races that are held frequently between April and November. As well as local Maltese events these include the Malta–Rimini Race and the famous Middle Sea Race around Sicily.

DIVING

This sea sport, a technical recreation not without its risks, has rapidly grown in popularity and the NTO provides detailed information and instructions on what is involved. Malta and Gozo have a number of fully licensed diving schools and as part of a well-developed infrastructure they belong to the Association of Professional Diving Schools, the other influential organisation being the Federation of Underwater Activities in Malta. Expert instruction is given, but anyone who wants to dive will need a permit issued by the Department of Health and this is dependent on a medical certificate vouching for physical fitness. The rest of the formalities can be left to the competent administration of the diving schools themselves.

The bold and rugged topographical features of the islands continue under water to provide a fascinating world of caves, grottos and crevices which offer ideal habitats for a varied and colourful assemblage of marine life. On Malta some of the main dive sites are at Ċirkewwa (Marfa Point), Aħrax Point, Anchor Bay, Merkanti Reef (off St Julian's Bay), Qawra Point, Għar Lapsi and Wied iż-Żurrieq. Reqqa Point, Dwejra Point and Mġarr ix-Xini (Ta' Ċenc)

Rocky limestone cliffs dominate much of Malta's south coast

are recommended Gozitan sites, as are Ras I' Irqeqa and St Marija Caves on Comino. Descriptions of the varied diving experiences at these 12 sites is given in the NTO literature and further fascination is the encounter of wrecks – ships and planes – which have been efficiently colonised by fauna and flora.

Divers will be relieved (or disappointed!) not to encounter 'big game' species, for sharks are rare, though in winter tuna, dolphin and bonito are sometimes spotted. The most common fauna are groupers, amberjacks, various bream and wrasse, damsel fish, octopus, squid, gurnard (gurnet), mullet, moray eel (more a night-time species) and others. Fascinating to watch, but dangerous to touch, are the scorpion fish, bristle worm (polychaete) and sting ray.

Diving has led to a number of ancillary activities including the 'Blue Dolphin of Malta', an underwater photographic competition organised by the FUAM. Experienced worldwide divers with their cameras participate in this challenging contest which is judged in November. Their photographs have greatly popularised the beauties of Malta's surrounding seas, as have those of the 'Mini Blue Dolphin' (introduced in 1989) where divers can submit the best of three photographs in a year.

Soccer

This, the undisputed national game, starts its official season in September, following the summer recess. The 'aficionada' turn out in style and there is much rowdyism, though nothing of the anti-social behaviour that often accompanies matches in other European countries. Most towns and many villages have teams competing in a number of divisions under the aegis of the Malta Football Association (tel: 222697). Premier Division matches and international games are played in the new National Stadium at Ta' Qali (near Rabat–Mdina), the lower division clubs using various grounds, Marsa in particular. The Maltese are also avid supporters of British and Italian teams.

Basketball

The popularity of this sport has greatly increased over the past few years and there is now a Basketball Association (tel: 499481) and League. The season begins in January and First Division teams attract large crowds to the Ta' Qali Sports Pavilion and other weekend venues.

The Marsa Sports Club

Easily reached from most parts of the Valletta conurbation, the Marsa complex (see page 116) epitomises the serious Maltese involvement with sport. Located here are tennis, squash and badminton courts, football pitches, a cricket ground, running track, polo field and swimming pool. Marsa is also the home of the Royal Malta Golf Club and the Malta Racing Club, which attracts large Sunday afternoon crowds to its regular flat races and trotting events. The centre welcomes visitors, though temporary membership charges are applicable. The complex also has a health and leisure centre with a fully equipped gymnasium and sauna facilities, and a well-appointed club house with restaurants, bars and lounge areas.

Other Sports and Events

First held on 16 February 1986, the Malta Marathon has become a successful annual event, attracting many overseas participants. The route covers the distance of 42 kilometres starting from the main gate of Mdina and finishing in Sliema. Other internationally supported events are the Malta and Gozo Motor Rally (held in November and covering a course of 240 kilometres) and the Malta Air Rally, currently in its twenty-first year. It features light aircraft from many parts of the world but chiefly from western Europe. National and international archery tournaments are also held, together with lawn tennis championships. Popular indoor sports include snooker and billiards, table tennis, darts and bowling, the venue for the latter being the large centre at Msida.

Hiking and Biking

The islands have become popular venues for ramblers and those who enjoy more strenuous hikes. With the help of a short ride by car or bus many areas can be explored on foot and *Landscapes of Malta, Gozo and Comino* by Lockhart & Ashton (see bibliography) is recommended for this purpose. Hiring a bicycle has many advantages but this activity can be strenuous under the hot summer sun and on Malta the traffic poses further difficulties. Gozitan traffic is lighter but the island is hillier.

Gaming and Lotteries

Betting on the Marsa horses, indeed on most things, is another Maltese passion. A popular game of chance is the weekly *Lotto* with its Friday prize draws but the largest payouts, if not quite 'retirement fortunes', come from the *National Grand Lottery* which is also an international sweepstake with prizes awarded four times a year. The frequency with which visitors win is naturally a contentious local issue. The ultimate in gaming sophistication is the Dragonara Palace Casino, once the home of Sir Hannibal Scicluna, Malta's Royal Librarian and eminent publicist. Unfortunately, this beautifully proportioned classical-style villa is vulgarised by neon advertising though its interior has preserved much of its former elegance. For this alone it is worth a visit and the palace has a sophisticated restaurant, bars and attractive gardens with a lido. The adventurous, of course, will be attracted to its gaming rooms which offer roulette, blackjack, baccarat and fruit machines. More down-market are Malta's bingo halls, many of them housed in old cinemas.

The Cinema

Like other European countries, the demise of the Maltese cinema is the concomitant of the popularity of television and the latter's strong diet of films, especially from Italian networks. Local newspapers carry lengthier columns on TV films than advertisements for the struggling cinemas left in Valletta and Sliema – the *Ambassador*, *Embassy*, *Gawhra*, *Gojjell* and *Alhambra*. These endeavour to screen the recent releases by international companies and most are in English, Maltese sub-titling being neither profitable nor needed.

Theatre and Concerts

These are usually well-supported and in addition to a

number of repertory companies the principal venue for theatrical activities is Valletta's Manoel Theatre (see page 106), dating from 1732 and claiming to be one of Europe's oldest live auditoriums. The theatre season runs from October to May and during the Christmas–New Year period the Manoel stages, in true Anglo–Maltese style, a traditional pantomime which attracts appreciative audiences of all ages. As Malta's national theatre, it also presents a varied repertoire of drama, ballet, opera and orchestral concerts by both Maltese and foreign companies. Lavish productions are tight fits on its eighteenth-century stage and even more clinical pruning is needed when companies tour provincial halls.

The Malta International Arts Festival ('Maltafest') is a major event held from mid-July to mid-August at various venues in Valletta, Floriana, the Three Cities and other towns. The 1990 festival featured international opera singers, orchestras, choirs and many exponents of fine and sculptured arts. The last weeks of November host the International Film and Video Festival, both receiving competitors and entries from all over the world.

✶ TOURING MALTA

1: Valletta and the Harbour Cities

Wedged between its twin natural harbours Valletta, in the words of Sir Walter Scott, 'is a splendid town, quite like a dream, rising majestically perpendicular from the water's edge to a height of eighty metres'. The reasons for its founding and the character of its planning were summarised on pages 74–75, and the Maltese are justly proud of their capital, an architectural and artistic masterpiece as well as being the administrative, commercial and cultural centre of Malta. It provides a treasure house of historical buildings and Disraeli was moved to describe it as 'a city of palaces built by gentlemen for gentlemen', for as well as perfecting its massive fortifications the Knights embellished it with grandiose edifices and monuments, a policy continued by the British. But observant visitors will also discover that Valletta has many contrasting streets and districts which offer, despite its limited boundaries, the same sociological strata as that found in cities of far greater size.

Walking is the best way to see the city, in fact it is the only means of access to many streets and quarters. Valletta's rectangular street grid makes orientation easy, and the detailed street map will enable visitors to plan their own itineraries. Inevitably these will start from City Gate, the main entrance from Floriana and the crowded Bus Station centred around the massive Triton Fountain, designed by Vincent Apap. Visitors first cross the mammoth dry ditch which physically separates Floriana from Valletta, and to the right is a lower access bridge of interest to railway enthusiasts for between 1883 and 1931 it carried the line from Mdina to Valletta station within the battlements. Replacing the old King's Gate, City Gate itself is a poor advertisement for what lies behind, for it was uninspiringly rebuilt in 1966 to accommodate modern access.

REPUBLIC STREET

The gate leads directly into Republic Street, the spine of the city leading north-east for 1.5 kilometres to Fort St Elmo. Containing many of Valletta's major sights, frequent changes of name – Strada San Giorgio, Rue de la Répub-

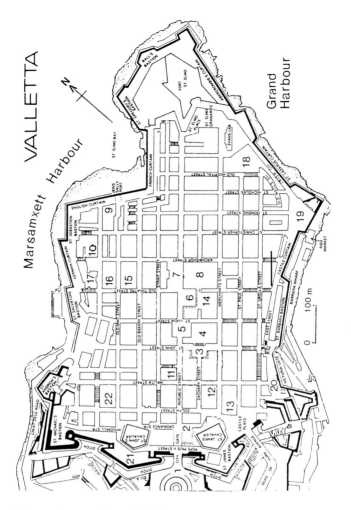

Map and street plan of Valletta

VALLETTA - Key to street plan

1. City Gate
2. Old Opera House
3. St John's Square
4. St John's Cathedral
5. Great Siege Square
6. Queen's Square
7. Palace Square
8. Grand Masters Palace
9. Auberge de Bavarie
10. Auberge d'Aragon
11. Auberge de Provence
12. Auberge d'Italie
13. Auberge de Castille
14. Royal Malta Library
15. Manoel Theatre
16. Carmelite Church
17. Anglican Cathedral
18. Hospital of the Knights
19. Lower Barracca Gardens
20. Upper Barracca Gardens
21. Hastings Gardens
22. Museum of Fine Arts

'The Gut' – Strait Street in Valletta – once a more notorious venue

lique (during the French occupation), Strada Reale and Kingsway – reflects much of the city's and Malta's history. Once inside the gate is the site (on the right) of the Royal Opera House, designed by Edward Barry (the architect of Covent Garden) and opened in 1866. It was regarded as one of Europe's most beautiful opera houses and functioned until World War II. Completely destroyed in the blitz its replacement has long been contemplated. Close by is Valletta's oldest church, Our Lady of the Victories, completed in 1567 to commemorate the first Great Siege.

Beyond the ruined opera house the real character of **Republic Street** begins, this shopping and business thoroughfare being the busiest in Malta. It is crowded throughout the day, but especially during the evening social stroll known as the *passaggiata*. The street is closed to traffic, except during the regulated shop delivery times. Along its course the street opens out into a series of squares – St John's Square, Great Siege Square, Queen's Square and Palace Square – each containing important historical buildings and some housing large pavement cafés which are integral parts of Valletta's social life.

With the location of Republic Street in mind, and also that of the second main artery, **Merchants Street**, visitors can begin their urban wanderings with confidence. But, in case it is missed, mention is given here to **Strait Street**, the narrow alley-like way paralleling Republic Street on its other side. This was better known to British servicemen as 'The Gut', the infamous home of bars, clubs and other nocturnal pleasures. Its function as a 'red-light' district is anything but new, for as long ago as 1554 an Italian writer had stressed the need for such a street as 'Strada Stretta', recommending that 'the brothel and similar taverns should be placed as near as possible to the main square, but carefully camouflaged'. Such is 'The Gut' today, this long, steep and narrow street being largely hidden, but its main centre of activity is located in close proximity to the Grand Masters Palace. Whether the knightly order, sworn to abstinence, frequented this quarter remains pure conjecture. Strait Street is now a shadow of its former commercial self, though its sleazy atmosphere remains. It is completely safe to walk along and enlightened visitors will enjoy the amusing repartee of the remaining and hardworking locals!

The following are further descriptions of the 'musts' of Valletta – those sights and experiences which no one should miss. They are presented in no particular order and visitors, planning their own tour, will find them all located on the street plan.

THE BASTIONS

Largely completed between 1566 and 1570 (though with major later additions and alterations), Valletta's complicated bastions and curtains (see page 75) are collectively one of the city's major points of interest. The names given to the many sections of this powerful enceinte are shown on the city plan, most of these fortifications built in typical zig-zag formation which, at the time of construction, provided the most effective means of citadel defence. Major repair work was undertaken in the 1970s and it is possible to walk the entire circuit of the defences either at street level or along the tops of many of them. Depending on the time taken to enjoy views over the city and harbours, visitors should allow themselves at least two hours. Seawards, Valletta's walls terminate at Fort St Elmo which was destroyed in the Ottoman siege, the present structure being largely the work of Laparelli and subsequent modifications, including British. Special permission is needed to visit the main sections of St Elmo, but visitors have access to the War Museum with its interesting displays of World War II and other military relics. The large open court on the fort's landward side is the paved covering of the old underground St Elmo granaries.

PALACE OF THE GRAND MASTERS

Located opposite Palace Square in Republic Street, but with other entrances from Merchants and Archbishop Streets this large, two-storey building offers austere façades at all approaches. Now the Presidential Office and Malta's Parliament House, it was once the administrative headquarters of the Grand Masters, the palace being an enlargement of a Valletta grand house, the reconstruction largely the work of Gerolamo Cassar. Further additions and improvements to this 'nerve-centre' of the knightly order were made by many Grand Masters and the long building is a repository of much of Malta's history. Within the formal exterior are two attractively green courtyards, **Prince Alfred's** and **Neptune's Courts**, the latter named after the bronze statue of the sea god, said to have been rescued from the old fish market in the seventeenth century. Many of the palatial rooms are open to visitors, including the splendid **Supreme Council Chamber** (now known as the Hall of St Michael and St George, for it was here that this chivalrous British order was founded), the Ambassador's Room (where foreign envoys are received), the Tapestry Room with its priceless woven hangings, and the Armoury containing the personal weapons and clothing at the time of the Knights.

THE AUBERGES

When the Knights moved from Birgu (Vittoriosa) to Valletta they commissioned the building of their langue auberges (see page 73), all designed by Cassar between 1571 and 1590, though many were subsequently altered. Only four of these original 'inns' survive, for those of France and Auvergne were destroyed during Malta's blitz and Allemagne (Ger-

(Above) The waterfront, Vittoriosa   (Below) Sunset, Valletta

(Above) An inner sanctuary, Ġgantija (Below) Main entrance
to Ħaġar Qim temple

Xlendi harbour. Gozo

many) was demolished in 1838 to make room for the building of the Anglican Cathedral of St Paul's. In 1783, when the Anglo–Bavarian language was formed what had previously been the Palazzo Carneric is now known as the **Auberge de Bavarie**. Used as a government department it overlooks Marsamxett Harbour close to St Elmo Fort.

The **Auberge d'Aragon**, a plain one-storey building with a Doric porch, was Cassar's first creation and it stands in Independence Square opposite St Paul's Cathedral. Much more impressive in Republic Street is the **Auberge**

The imposing Auberge de Castille et Leon overlooking Castille Place was built by Cassar and remodelled by Cachia

de Provence whose ornate classical entrance also carries the langue's coat-of-arms. It now houses the **National Museum of Archaeology**, the large halls of this inn, with wooden ceilings and beautifully painted walls, being the exhibition areas for the comprehensive collection of artefacts from Malta's prehistoric and later archaeological sites.

In Merchants Street the **Auberge d'Italie** was much enlarged in the seventeenth century during the grand mastership of Carafa, whose bust and detailed enblazature adorns its main entrance. Used as Law Courts by the British, it is now Valletta's main post office. But by far the finest of the auberge-palaces is the **Auberge de Castille and Leon** which presides over Castille Place at Valletta's southeast battlements. Remodelled in 1744 during the time of Grand Master Pinto (whose bust with carved banners and war implements sits above the entrance), this magnificently ornate structure with symmetrical window sequences makes it, arguably, one of Malta's finest buildings.

ST JOHN'S CO-CATHEDRAL

A product of Cassar's architectural ingenuity, St John's was built as the Coventual Church of the Knights and consecrated in 1578. Compared to the later high Baroque façades of other island churches, large and small, its exterior is plain and sombre, and closely surrounded by other buildings, its townscape impact is limited. It is best approached from Zachary Street which reaches **St John's Square** through an arched way, but even from this angle the entrance to what is Malta's co-cathedral (see page 135) is austere, the attendant square bell-towers adding to its battlemented appearance. But visitors will soon realise that an important characteristic of Maltese architecture, monumental or purely domestic, is a plain, solidly built exterior which hides from the street attractive and, in the case of churches, richly decorated interiors. St John's is no exception and those seeing it for the first time should prepare themselves for a dazzling experience of light and colour, its decorations and monuments providing magnificent reminders of the opulent history of the islands under the rule of the Knights.

Basically rectangular in shape, the church is roofed by a huge barrel vault segmented into panels gloriously decorated by the oil on stone frescoes of Mattia Preti. In true Michaelangelo style it took him five years to complete this ceiling, the theme being the story of St John the Baptist, though also illustrating other saints and heroes of the Order. Discovering the islands, visitors will come across other works of Preti (1613–99), a native of Calabria who studied in

Naples before working in Rome under the influence of the Caravaggio School. After travelling Europe he settled in Malta and from 1661 onwards became the Order's chief ecclesiastical decorator. As well as frescoes, his artistic output included numerous canvasses, altarpieces and other works of religious art. Many have criticised the variable quality of his work, but few would disagree that the ceiling of St John's is one of his masterpieces.

Symmetrically arranged on either side of the main body of the church are the chapels of the *langues*, arranged as bays. All are magnificently decorated and contain valuable paintings and other treasures. It would be hard to find one square inch of this church not painted, gilded or carved, and its decoration also includes the polychrome slabs which cover the cathedral's floor, each marking the tomb of an influential knight or another dignatory identified by their personal insignia. Yet none of this flamboyance distracts from the church's focal point, the High Altar, fashioned in rare marbles, lapis lazuli and gilded ornamentation, all to the design of Lorenzo Gafà.

The crypt of St John's is entered from the Chapel of Provence and has tombs of the early Grand Masters, including de L'Isle-Adam who brought the Order to the islands. Annexed to the co-cathedral is a museum which houses silverware, embroidered vestments, tapestries and paintings, many of which are paraded on religious feasts and other celebratory days.

GREAT SIEGE AND QUEEN'S SQUARES

Some third of the way along Republic Street from City Gate is **Great Siege Square** with a monument designed by the Maltese sculptor, Antonio Sciortino. The three figures of Courage, Liberty and Religion commemorate Malta's victory over the Turks in 1565. On the square's west side is the Law Courts, a classical edifice built in 1967 on the site of the bombed Auberge de Auvergne.

A block away is **Queen's Square**, an attractive tree-lined area fronting the **Royal Malta Library**, locally known as 'the Bibliotheca'. It was completed in 1796 during the grand mastership of de Rohan as a depository of the Order's books and manuscripts, these now being priceless archives, especially the collection on incunabula (books printed before 1500). The library also has records of the old *Università* (see page 71) and currently functions as one of Malta's main reference and research institutions. Presided over by a typically non-amused statue of Queen Victoria the square's large pavement cafés are, nonetheless, the main centre of

Pavement cafés play a prominent role in Valletta's social life

relaxation for what might appear to be the entire population of Valletta and its visitors.

THE MANOEL THEATRE AND ANGLICAN CHURCH

Where Queen's and Palace Squares meet, Old Theatre Street drops down to the defences along this part of Marsamxett Harbour. On the right is the **Manoel Theatre**, built in 1731 and named after Grand Master Manoel de Vilhena. It suffered much competition when the Opera

House was opened and for a time was a refuge for down-and-outs, and then a cinema. In 1960 it was sympathetically restored to serve as the National Theatre (see page 96) and it is open to visitors during the day, though times are restricted.

Close by is the **Church of Our Lady of Mount Carmel** whose huge new dome dominates the view of Valletta from Sliema. Its rebuilding follows severe bomb damage and like many Maltese churches the enlarged fabric has been built around an older one. Its interior walls await painting and other adornment, their present bareness emphasising its massive proportions and 138-foot high dome. Around the corner in Independence Square is the **Anglican Cathedral of St Paul's**, designed by Richard Lankersheer and built by William Scamp in 1839–41, the money coming from Queen Adelaide, widow of William IV. Its high Gothic-style spire, another landmark from Sliema, cleverly blends with the classical proportions of the main façade.

THE HOSPITAL OF THE KNIGHTS

This massive building, located to the north of St Lazarus Curtain and close to Fort St Elmo, was renovated in 1979 to provide Valletta with a modern conference and exhibition complex. Originally the Sacra Infermia or Holy Hospital built in 1574, the structure is one of the oldest surviving hospital buildings in Europe with a single-roofed hall purported to be the longest in the world. The modern centre now incorporates five large venues suitable for all types of meetings, displays, concerts and theatrical performances. Popular with visitors is the 'Malta Experience', a multivision spectacle dealing with the history and modern lifestyle of the islands.

THE PUBLIC GARDENS

Congested Valletta has few areas of open space and those that exist, albeit small, offer pleasant places for relaxation. Built into the great battlements they also offer splendid panoramas, especially the Lower and Upper Barracca Gardens with their views over the Three Cities (see below) and the animated creeks of the Grand Harbour. Both are well laid out with trees and shrubs and contain interesting monuments, though chiefly to British notables. Another garden, Hastings, is set in the battlements overlooking Floriana. Its name commemorates Malta's second British Governor.

Other Valletta Sights

As noted, the above descriptions have highlighted only the main sights of the city and the intrepid visitor will discover much more that is of interest. There are numerous other city houses of palatial proportions and a wealth of beautiful churches and chapels by Cassar, Barbara and other Maltese architects, their interiors also rich in ecclesiastical art. If appetites are still keen the **National Museum of Fine Arts** (in South Street towards Marsamxett Harbour) provides a collection of works by Maltese painters and various pieces from Italian, Flemish and other schools.

Valletta is a city that oozes the past and to know it demands time. It has been called 'the city with a soul' and much of this is governed by the fact that its original character is now being actively maintained.

Floriana

Built as a fortified suburb (see page 75) to strengthen Valletta's landward defences, the main route into Floriana (and on to Valletta) is through the **Portes des Bombes**, a monumental double-arched gateway built in two stages. The earlier section dates from 1721 and the grand-mastership of Ramon Perellos and was erected to commemorate further successful actions against the Ottomans. The Latin inscription reads: 'Safely I am at home while I fight the Turks everywhere'. Built some 150 years later an identical archway carries a more mundane British message: 'For the convenience of the people – 1868'.

Entering the battlements, the road diverges to the left to become St Anne's Street, Floriana's main thoroughfare. On the right and protected by a central bastion is the **Argotti Botanic Garden**, containing many rare and exotic species together with an interesting cacti collection. These bastions form the settings for other attractive gardens and nurseries, and leading from them through the centre of Floriana to City Gate are broad avenues – The Mall and Sarria Street – which between them bound the **Maglio Gardens**. Laid out in 1656, this was once a walled enclosure used by the Knights to play *pallamaglio* (pall-mall), the theory being that healthy exercise would detract their thoughts from temptations of the flesh. This linear garden has many monuments to distinguished Maltese citizens and the small fountain commemorates the completion of the aqueduct by which Grand Master Alof de Wignacourt (see page 129) provided water for Valletta. On one side of the gardens is a sports arena – an old parade ground – and the other is occupied by underground, bottle-shaped granaries similar

The church of St Publius and underground granaries, Floriana

to those of St Elmo. This large paved area fronts the impressive twin-towered church of **St Publius**, dating from 1733 but remodelled in 1882 and now fully restored after severe bomb damage.

Within its defences, Floriana's building area more than matched that of Valletta's, yet the city was never fully developed and for visitors re-entering from Valletta its open spaces provide a real breath of openness and fresh air. Some impression of what the entire city might have looked like is provided by the broad arcaded stretch of St Anne's Street and the grid-patterned thoroughfares leading off it. But, despite some elegant architecture and the presence of prestigious embassies, its general atmosphere is somewhat faded.

The Three Cities

Across the Grand Harbour from Valletta are the fortress towns of Senglea, Cospicua and Vittoriosa where the Knights first settled on Malta before moving their head-quarters to Valletta. Napoleon is credited with dubbing them the 'Three Cities' and they bore the brunt of destruction during the war, being directly in the target area around the dockyards. All three are easily reached from City Gate or by *dgħajsa* ride (see page 18) from Valletta's Customs House Wharf.

Named after Grand Master Claude de la Sengle (1553–1557) who fortified the peninsula between Dockyard and French Creeks, **Senglea** is also known as L'Isla. It was completely bombed out during the war and, for a time, was evacuated. It would be easy to criticise its uninspired modern style, but visitors should remember both the scale and urgency of post-war Malta's rebuilding programme. Some sections of the battlements remain and one structure that survived the blitz – for it was dismantled and then rebuilt – is the vedette (look-out tower) at Senglea Point which, with sculptured eye and ear, still provides impressive views across the harbour to Valletta.

Built in 1682, the parish church of Our Lady of Victories was almost completely destroyed, but has now been restored to its former ornate glory.

Bormla was the old name for **Cospicua**, the latter meaning 'Conspicuous', an honour given to it for the vital role it played at the time of the Turkish siege. Located at the inner part of Dockyard Creek and linking Senglea and Vittoriosa, it was also savagely bombed. Its rebuilding followed the old plan of narrow streets and alleys, many rising from the harbour area in flights of steps. Other than the modern dockyard activities, Cospicua's most interesting features are the great land defences known as the Margherita and Cottonera Lines. The former are a series of inner bastions begun in 1639, and the latter was an even more grandiose defensive project of outer bastions, ravelins and walls built as a massive semi-circular defence. Personally financed by Grand Master Niccola Cotoner (1663–80), the Cottonera Lines were designed to shelter some 40,000 people and their livestock. But they were neither fully completed nor militarily tested. Cospicua's other attraction is the fabulously opulent church of the Immaculate Conception.

Known as Birgu and re-christened **Vittoriosa** after the Turkish siege, this was the Order's first home on Malta, their security resting on a water-bounded location and the great Fort St Angelo which impressively rises out of the Grand Harbour at the tip of the narrowing peninsula. Vittoriosa has much to interest the visitor, not least its beautiful St Lawrence Church overlooking Dockyard Creek. Close by is Freedom Monument, a statuary group on a landscaped rock rises depicting a bugler, a man attending the Maltese flag and a British sailor saying farewell to a dockyard worker. Unveiled on 31 March 1979, it is a poignant epitaph to the spirit of friendship which marked Britain's withdrawal from the islands.

With the exception of Fort St Angelo and the adjacent Auberge d'Italie, Vittoriosa's other historical buildings are located at the wider, landward end of the city. The main palaces, churches and other places of interest are shown on the accompanying map.

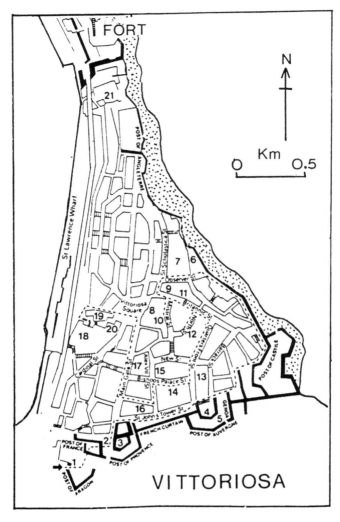

Street plan of Vittoriosa and suggested tour

1. Advance Gate
2. Main Gate
3. St John's Cavalier
4. St James' Cavalier
5. Gate of Auvergne
6. Infirmary Sally Port
7. Hospital of the Order
8. Auberge d'Allemagne
9. Auberge d'Auvergne et Provence
10. Auberge d'Angleterre
11. Auberge de France
12. Norman House
13. Armoury
14. Bishop's Palace
15. Residence of the Order's Chaplains
16. Palace of the Università
17. Inquisitors Palace
18. St Lawrence Church
19. Oratory of the Holy Crucifix
20. Oratory of St Joseph
21. Auberge d'Italie

Sliema – St Julian's

The towns on the opposite side of Marsamxett Harbour from Valletta are largely modern creations, many of them of twentieth-century growth and continually expanding. Via Portes des Bombes, the routes out of Floriana are detailed on pages 114–5 and buses to and from City Gate and various parts of Sliema are frequent throughout the day. From The Strand in Sliema (see below) Valletta is geographically close, but only as the crow flies, and visitors opting to walk between the two centres should note that the distance by land entails in excess of one hour's dedicated slog, an exhausting venture in Malta's summer heat. But at other times of the year it is highly recommended for a main road with pavement access hugs the shore of Marsamxett, snaking its way around the harbour's side creeks – Sliema, Lazzaretto, Msida and Pietà – before climbing inland to reach the Floriana defences. Whether from Sliema or Valletta–Floriana, visitors will pass **Manoel Island** with its boat-building yards and Phoenician Glass factory, the up-market marina in Lazzaretto and Msida Creeks, Msida's imposing parish church of St Joseph and the Sa Maison Gardens, close to where the Gozo ferry leaves.

SLIEMA

The largest component (population 30,000) of the Valletta conurbation, Sliema is also Malta's main tourist and most fashionable residential area, the product of nineteenth-century and modern growth. **The Tigne headland**, however, has long been strategically important in guarding

The boatyard at Manoel Island

Il Fortizza, Tower Road, Sliema

Marsamxett Harbour and its fort, dating from 1793, was the last of the main defensive works constructed by the Knights. Close by, though destroyed in the French troubles, stood the church of Our Lady of the Victories and Sliema gets its name from *Sliem*, meaning 'Hail', by which sailors saluted the church on entering and leaving the harbour. Other forts punctuate Sliema's northern coastline and formed part of a chain of seventeenth-century lookouts. The largest on Tower Road, **Il Fortizza**, is now a restaurant complex.

Tower Road is one of Sliema's main seafronts with a major concentration of hotels, apartment houses, restaurants and bars. It is quieter and more sophisticated than its other esplanade, **The Strand** and its continuation as **Tigne Sea Front**, where a decidedly commercialised atmosphere pervades. These two promenades are linked by a series of short and, in places, steep streets which form the town's centre with a large collection of banks, tourist offices, and shops.

Those who regard Sliema as architecturally undistinguished have probably ventured little further than its waterside locations. The town's real character awaits discovery in the maze of streets and by-roads that lie behind the seafronts. Though lacking in buildings of major historical importance the parish churches and chapels are equally opulent and Sliema's solidly built stone homes, with their individualistic balconies and personalised doors are among the most attractively grand on Malta. It is unfortunate that the architectural uniformity of many streets has been sacrificed to modern high-rise commercial premises, though the conservationists are active in their battle against further townscape damage.

ST JULIAN'S

The seafront walk from Sliema to its acolyte, St Julian's, is especially attractive. Extending around St Julian's Point and its watchtower, Tower Road becomes the main street which circuits the shore of Balluta Bay. Rounding the headland St Julian's Bay is reached, its old fishing village having rapidly succumbed to tourism, though at its inner part – **Spinola Bay** – many colourful and authentic vestiges of the past remain. Paceville (Il-Qaliet), an extension of St Julian's, has become a busy shopping and night-life centre, aided by the presence of Malta's Hilton and the Dragonara Palace Casino (see page 96). **St Julian's–Paceville** has many of Malta's fast-food chains and ethnic restaurants. The coast offers rocky bathing and a wealth of organised water sports, and its bars and discotheques keep late hours. The pace of development along this section of Malta's coast shows little sign of abatement, the most recent area of commercialisation being **St George's Bay**, graced with a tiny sandy beach. St Julian's is the gateway for the popular excursion along the island's northern coast (see page 143).

The island itineraries that follow use Valletta's City Gate as a starting point, for the majority of venues discussed are accessible by public transport. As noted, private car offers the most flexible means of touring, but the towns, main villages and the majority of historical and scenic places noted below have been visited by the author on local buses. Admittedly this has demanded a number of holidays and has also entailed a considerable amount of enjoyable walking to and from countryside termini.

Appendix 3 provides a map of the main island's bus routes together with an alphabetical list of major destinations and their respective bus numbers. In reality the system is more complex, for further services, chiefly to popular coastal and scenic venues, operate in summer and visitors will also discover a number of useful inter-town and -village links. The Despatcher's Kiosk (see page 15) will provide up-to-date information. The map (see page 165) summarises the routes described, but visitors are recommended to purchase a good topographical map.

Out of City Gate and Floriana, much of the main traffic is directed through Portes des Bombes, after which a series of busy interchanges deflects it to various destinations. At

The impressive townscape of Floriana viewed from St James Cavalier, Valletta

the first main junction traffic is funnelled off to the Sliema area (via Gwardamanga–Pietà and Msida) and a short distance to the southwest is the Ħamrun roundabout which controls most of the traffic to central and north-western Malta. South again, a series of interchanges at Marsa, particularly the two bounding its industrial estate, are the foci of routes for south-eastern and southern parts of the island.

2: South-East Malta

Route 1 : Marsa – Żabbar – The East Coast – Marsaskala – Delimara Point

Marsa is situated at the head of Newport or Marsa Creek,

Msida church and creek – now part of a large marina

the innermost part of the Grand Harbour. It is an important industrial sector of the Valletta conurbation with activities based on the dockyards and the large industrial estate. Most visitors use Marsa for its sports centre (see page 95) or as a gateway to the countryside and coasts of southern and eastern Malta. From the industrial estate, the road to Żabbar and Marsaskala skirts the centre of Paola (see below) and continues through the expanding townships of Għajn Dwieli and Fgura. A little beyond the junction for Żejtun, the approach to Żabbar is marked by a triumphal arch built in honour of Grand Master Ferdinand von Hompesch. It carries the distinction of being the last monumental structure erected by the Knights on Malta.

ŻABBAR

This large agricultural and residential town, one of the early *casals*, has a population in excess of 13,000. It grew to prominence in the seventeenth century when, with the danger of pirate raids diminished, it became an overspill settlement to the south-east of the Three Cities. It was linked to these by the splendid **Żabbar Gate** in the Cottonera Lines, but exclusion from the main fortifications was to cause problems and Żabbar was destined to play a major role in Malta's military history. The town was one of the main bases of operations by Maltese insurgents against the French who had lodged themselves behind the Valletta Floriana and Cottonera defences.

Within canon range of the latter, it was inevitable that Żabbar was seriously damaged, a major architectural victim being the church of **Our Lady of the Graces**. Begun by Dingli in 1641 and probably completed by others, including Gafà to whom the dome is often attributed, the church has been fully restored. Dingli's original nave ceiling is of major interest and a small museum contains rich treasures, including votive paintings depicting miraculous escapes from piracy and other dangers. The town's small church of **St Dominica** is an important illustration of pre-Order ecclesiastical architecture.

RICASOLI FORT TO ŻONQOR POINT

A number of roads radiate from Żabbar and an interesting itinerary is one which first heads north-westwards through the Żabbar Gate to circuit the inner side of the Cottonera Lines. Passing the prestigious St Edward's and De la Salle Colleges, the road leaves the enceinte via Salvatore Gate where it descends to **Kalkara**, still a picturesque area (despite modern additions), built around its creek. This was once the harbour for galleys of the Langue of England, hence its other name, English Creek. Crossing the neck of the squat Bighi peninsula to Rinella Creek the massive structures of **Ricasoli Fort** lie ahead. Now largely derelict, this heavily defended promontory was the counterpart of Fort St Elmo across the narrow entrance to the Grand Harbour.

Lined with other forts and defensive installations, the stretch of coastline from Ricasoli south-eastwards to Żonqor Point and Marsaskala Bay provides an attractive and easily negotiable walk, the distance from San Rocco on the outskirts of Kalkara (bus access from Valletta) being some 7 kilometres. The limestone cliffs are picturesque rather than spectacular and in springtime their crumbling descents to the sea and attendant farmlands behind are a riot of floral colour. The path first leads to the small village of **Xgħajra** where bathing is possible from a rocky foreshore. Passing Fort Leonardo and a coastal look-out tower, **Żonqor Point** is reached where another fort dramatically guards the entrance to Marsaskala Bay. For the motorist this coastal path is paralleled (some 0.5 kilometres inland) by a rural road from Rinella, via San Rocco, to Marsaskala.

MARSASKALA

Built around the head of its long sea inlet, Marsaskala is an old-style fishing and farming village now undergoing rapid transformation as a tourist venue. A number of popular restaurants fringe the rocky shore and modern ribbon development extends around the southern-bounding Il-Gżira headland. Here the **St Thomas Tower** (built in 1614) has been converted into a fashionable eating place and close by are new hotels, including the 4-star **Jerma Palace**, its 350-room capacity ensuring the Marsaskala area of a large number of year-round visitors.

A more direct route (less than 3 kilometres) links Żabbar to Marsaskala which is also easily reached from Żejtun (see page 119), this road first reaching the **St Thomas Bay** area. Lying to the south of Marsaskala, between Miġnuna Point and Il-Munxar headland, and protected out to sea by Munxar Reef (a notorious hazard to early shipping), the coves of St Thomas Bay appear ripe for tourist development.

THE DELIMARA PENINSULA

A more exciting, but in many places difficult walk is

southwards along the finger-like peninsula from Marsaskala Bay to **Delimara Point**, which bounds Marsaxlokk Bay to the east (see page 120). This coastal tract (rough distance 8 kilometres) is one of rugged limestone headlands and a succession of semi-circular, cliff-fringed bays undergoing active wave attack. The many landslips and loss of valuable farmland to the sea is readily apparent and great care is needed when following what appears to be a safe pathway marked on maps. Another hazard (see page 55) is the popularity of Delimara with the insidious bird-shooters.

South from St Thomas Bay and the needle-pointed Il-Munxar promontory, the next rugged headland is **Xrobb il-Għaġin** whose approach is marked by a forlornly situated country chapel dedicated to St Paul. Nearby are some poor vestiges of prehistoric temples which need to be searched for in this rocky, overgrown area. From Xrobb il-Għaġin the view southwards takes in two large bays – **Hofra L-Kbria** and **Hofra iz-Żgwira** – separated by another pencil-thin promontory Ras il-Fenek, in imminent danger of destruction by the sea. To the west and once controlling the Delimara approaches is the Tas Silġ Battery (largely hidden by vegetation) and close to it is Tas Silġ church at a road junction that leads to Marsaxlokk. As noted in earlier pages, this part of the island has a number of ancient, but unspectacular remains. Continuing southwards through this narrowing, bay-etched peninsula the path, which now joins a minor road, passes Fort Delimara to reach the lighthouse close to Delimara Point. The latter part of this Delimara walk can more easily be made from Marsaxlokk.

Route 2 : Paola – Tarxien – Żejtun – Marsaxlokk – Birżebbuġa – Għar Hasan

PAOLA

The eastern interchange at the Marsa industrial estate is also one of the main approaches to **Paola** (or Pawla), another rapidly expanding adjunct to the Valletta conurbation with a population of 12,000. Most people visit it for the **Hal Saflieni hypogeum** (see page 63), but the town has much more to offer, especially for those interested in Renaissance town planning. Unlike the traditional Maltese *casals*, its most notable urban characteristic is its regular grid of straight, broad streets.

The original plan was instigated by Grand Master Antoine de Paule (1623–36) who christened it Casal Nuova, a fitting name for what was conceived as a seventeenth-

(Above) Ramla Bay, Gozo   (Below) Lacemaker in Victoria, Gozo

(Above) Pietà Creek and Floriana's defences   (Below) The
north-west coast at Marfa Point   (Bottom) Fishing harbour,
St Julian's

century new town to relieve the overcrowding problems of Valletta and the Three Cities. Its site was an area of higher ground to the south of the Grand Harbour and great thought was given to the compass alignment of its parallel streets, those trending in a general north-south direction pointing to the fortifications of Valletta, with the transverse streets lined up to view the distant dome of Mdina cathedral. As well as being symbolic, this pattern allowed for the penetration of cool breezes from the north and west. But Paola's initial success was limited, for few Maltese were confident to move beyond the girded protection of the Grand Harbour cities.

As part of the original plan the parish church of **St Ubaldesca** was designed by Vittorio Cassar, but by the beginning of this century Paola's growth and prosperity warranted a new church and Guzè Damato (1886–1958) was commissioned to build **Christ the King**, his work commencing in 1924. It took the form of a Neo-Romanesque structure with twin-domed towers framing an ornately porticoed front, its interior being equally individualistic and impressive. Born of Maltese parents in Sfax (Tunisia), Damato's work is seen in other parts of the islands, including the parish church of St John the Baptist at Xewkija on Gozo.

TARXIEN

Presided over by Damato's church, Paola's busy main street, the scene of a large open-air market, is part of the main traffic route to adjoining **Tarxien**, the road passing close to the famous temple ruins (see page 64). The ordered structure of Paola quickly reverts to one of narrow, winding streets and alleys, for Tarxien (population 8,000) is essentially an old agricultural village. Other than its antiquities its main point of interest is the richly monumental parish church whose symmetrical belfry-towers front an extra wide main body.

ŻEJTUN

From Tarxien the main road to **Żejtun** (12,000 inhabitants) crosses fertile farmlands. This is a town of considerable history with Punic and earlier remains in its vicinity and modest Roman structures recently unearthed in the grounds of the local girls' school. Sacked by the Turks in 1436, Żejtun was solidly rebuilt and became the administrative centre for south-east Malta. Begun in 1692 **St Catherine's** is regarded as Gafà's finest parish church and preserves much of its seventeenth-century classical elegance. It presides over an irregular square, the focus of Żejtun's maze of little streets which entice one to explore. Here to be discovered is **St Gregory's**, one of Malta's few surviving medieval churches to which the Knights added a Renaissance doorway, bell-cote and a larger transcept. Secret recesses in its walls were found to contain scores of skeletons and the church is a noted place of pilgrimage.

From Żejtun roads fan out in all directions – to Żabbar, Marsaskala and St Thomas Bay, and to Marsaxlokk and Birżebbuġa, the latter destinations more easily reached from the Bir-id-Deheb crossroads (see page 123).

MARSAXLOKK

Marsaxlokk lies at the head of the eastern arm of the irregularly-shaped Marsaxlokk Bay which, between Delimara Point and Bengħisa Point bites deeply and widely into Malta's south-east coast. As noted, this has been a vulnerable entry point for the island and its headlands have remains of ancient settlements together with fortifications of medieval and later times. Here Suleiman's fleet disembarked in 1565 and fought their first battle with the Knights at Żejtun. The bay also witnessed the arrival of part of Napoleon's armada.

Marsaxlokk, a Maltese corruption of Marsascirocco (Arabic *marsa* meaning 'harbour', and Sicilian *scirocco*, meaning 'south wind') is the largest of Malta's traditional fishing villages and, many would argue, the most attractive. Full of brightly-painted *luzzu* boats, it is popular with artists and photographers and other authentic colour comes from pastel-painted houses that line the waterfront, many of

Work on a Maltese *Luzzu* Marsaxlokk

Part of the fishing fleet in Marsaxlokk Harbour

them having attractive doors and fanlights. Here fishermen mend their boats, nets and traps while the women and girls tend stalls selling colourful bags, lace cloths and other locally-produced items.

The oldest part of the village lies adjacent to the prominent parish church whose twin front towers and octagonal red-roofed dome (sometimes repainted blue) occupy raised ground at the inner part of the harbour. Close by are old cottages and boathouses but the local fish market is animated for a short time only, for the valuable catch is quickly dispersed to urban destinations. Surrounded by new villas and apartment blocks in the south-western part of the village is **Kavallerizza**, an imposing structure which was once an equestrian training school for the Knights.

The Delimara promontory (see Route 1) is easily reached from Marsaxlokk and a shorter version of the coastal walk can be made from the village.

BIRŻEBBUĠA

Southwards out of Marsaxlokk the road to Birżebbuġa skirts the great bay's squat central peninsula ending in **Il Ponta l-Kbira** with a short stretch of sand. Built in 1610 to guard this strategic headland, the monolithic fortress of **St Lucian** is a major local landmark and it appears to have been the only island defence where the Knights gave the invading French some opposition. It retained its military function under the British but has since served as a marine sciences laboratory actively involved in Mediterranean pollution projects.

Further defences fringe the shore of what now becomes

St George's Bay, bounded on the south-west by the circular-shaped promontory where Birżebbuġa stands. Reaching the sandy stretch at the innermost part of this bay is the direct road from Bir-id-Deheb which descends to the eastern side of **Wied Dalam** with its many prehistoric and other early remains (see page 61).

Meaning 'Well of the Olives', **Birżebbuġa** has lost much of its former charm for this old fishing village turned seaside resort has become embroiled in the development of Freeport Malta (see page 88). Formerly attractive coastal views are now scarred by oil and other storage facilities, together with a massive breakwater providing berth for the largest of bulk carriers. On the southern side of the town and once the haunt of well-off Maltese families is **Pretty Bay**, a description now hardly applicable though its restaurants and bars remain popular. The bay extends south-eastwards to **Kalafrana** where the old RAF sea-plane base forms part of the development zone.

GHAR HASAN

Many parts of the island's south coast are easily reached from Birżebbuġa and a popular local attraction is **Għar Hasan** (Cave of Hasan). This dark labyrinth of limestone passageways is reached by a pathway and steps cut into a high cliff face. For a modest fee visitors without torches can hire them from the self-styled 'guide', but claustrophobics should give this speleological adventure a miss. Of the many legends about Hasan, all refer to him as a Saracen who took refuge here when the Arabs were driven from Malta. One version tells of the Maltese maiden he is said to have abducted, and when their hiding place was discovered both Hasan and his captive leapt to their death into the sea.

Back on the main road at the turn-off to the cave, the route to the west skirts the northern side of Hal Far airfield to a main junction. Here one road leads to Żurrieq and the other continues north-westwards to Luqa and Valletta.

3: South–Central Malta

Route 3 : Luqa – Gudja and Għaxaq – Mqabba and Qrendi – Żurrieq – Blue Grotto

From the western interchange at Marsa's industrial estate the main routes south first focus on Luqa which, with Malta's airport close by is a major island route centre. To the east is the prominent **Addolorata Cemetery**, the resting place of many rich and notable Maltese citizens. Both architecturally and historically it is a fascinating venue to visit for its grandiose monuments and magnanimous epitaphs provide an illuminating summary of important personalities that have helped to fashion the island's character.

LUQA

Much of this south-bound traffic skirts **Luqa**, the town itself being somewhat nondescript and attracting few visitors for it suffered the same devastation that afflicted its airfield during World War II. But it does boast two interesting churches, that of the Assumption, dating from the fifteenth century and the totally rebuilt St Andrew's which incorporates the original altarpieces of Mattia Preti.

GUDJA AND GĦAXAQ

Before the southern route tunnels beneath Luqa's main runway, a road to the left leads to the farming villages of Gudja and Għaxaq and, via Bir id-Deheb, on to Żejtun. Gudja takes pride in being the birthplace of Geralomo Cassar and contains an interesting collection of buildings, including the seventeenth-century church of the Virgin of Loreto, distinguished by its impressive dome and loggia. A little to the north-west of the village centre is Ta' Bir Miftuħ (St Mary of the Open Well) built in 1436 when it was a focus of one of Malta's original parishes. Between Gudja and **Għaxaq**, at Ix-Xlejli, is the late eighteenth-century **Dorrel Palace** (or Villa Bettina) which entertained both Napoleon and Nelson. Għaxaq is a larger village and, via Bir id-Deheb, merges with Żetjun. Its chief attraction is the church of St Mary.

MQABBA AND QRENDI

Beyond Luqa a complicated rural road pattern, leading to Żurrieq, also serves **Kirkop** and **Safi** to the east (now increasingly dependent on the job opportunities at the airport) and, to the west, the stone quarrying villages of Mqabba and Qrendi. The huge **Mqabba** quarries are a stopping point on many excursions and visitors can witness the relative ease by which Malta's main building material is cut and shaped. Despite this heavy activity Mqabba is a clean and attractive settlement of some 3,000 inhabitants, and particularly pleasing is its church of St Basil and many old homes with Moorish-style decorations. On its southern edge, at **Tal Mentna**, are early Christian catacombs, some

Rugged limestone outcrops and small terraced fields are found throughout Malta

of the tombs intricately decorated with scallop shell reliefs.

Those with a further appetite for Maltese churches will find plenty to interest them in the old village of **Qrendi** with its parish church of St Mary, the smaller St Saviour and, on the village's northern edge, the diminutive St Catherine Tat-Torba with its Baroque doorway and circular window. Qrendi's other features of interest include the **Gwarena Tower**, whose octagonal shape makes it unique to Malta, and the natural curiosity of **Il-Maqluba** meaning 'turned upside down'. Located to the south of the village this large (100 metres wide by 50 metres deep) limestone sink hole is the result of both surface erosion and the collapse of an underground cave system. It lies at the head of the rugged *wied* system which reaches this part of Malta's coast as the Blue Grotto (see below). In close proximity of Qrendi are the prehistoric temples of Hagar Qim and Mnajdra.

ŻURRIEQ

This attractive old *casal* at the head of Wied Babu is within easy walking distance of Qrendi. It is the main market town for the district and supports a population of over 8,000. Suffering from later additions and alterations, the main fabric of its parish church of St Catherine dates from 1675 and it houses an important collection of the works of Mattia Preti. Converted to a private palace in 1784, Zurrieq's **Armeria** was originally an Armoury for the Knights serving the many watchtowers that guarded this part of Malta's coast. The remnants of old corn mills also indicate the Order's preoccupation with profitable agriculture and many of them belong to the time (late seventeenth and early eighteenth centuries) when the Knights had a monopoly on their erection. This often led to the rapid expansion of the *casal* centres at the expense of smaller settlements, many declining and some becoming deserted. Such was the fate of **Hal Millieri** to the north of Żurrieq where all that remains is its late medieval church, now restored by Malta's active Conservation Society.

THE BLUE GROTTO

For many visitors this is one of the main scenic experiences of Malta. The **Blue Grotto** can be reached from Żurrieq and Qrendi, or by direct bus from City Gate. At the small coastal hamlet of **Wied iz-Żurrieq** fishermen in their brightly-painted boats conduct visitors, weather permitting, through a series of natural sea caves with multicoloured rock formations, the trip lasting some 25 minutes. Experts recommend a morning visit when the light is said to be at its best, enhancing the beauty of the grotto by reflecting off its white sandy bottom through the shimmering azure water. In summertime the queues are usually lengthy and visitors should note that priority is given to those on conducted tours, the operators having reserved boats in advance.

Wied iz-Żurrieq can be used as a start for a number of coastal walks westwards along the impressively steep southern edges of Malta. Highlights on route include the Hagar Qim and Mnajdra temples and Għar Lapsi (see below), from where paths continue on to the majestic Dingli Cliffs.

Route 4 : Qormi – Żebbug – Siġġiewi – Għar Lapsi

From the Marsa roundabout this route first leads westwards to Qormi, passing the Sports Centre which is built on flat land that was once an inland extension of the Grand Harbour. Qormi is quickly reached and then Żebbug where the route leads southwards to Siġġiewi and continues to Għar Lapsi on the south coast.

QORMI

Now also part of the Valletta conurbation and joined to Marsa and Hamrun, **Qormi** is a flourishing town with a population of over 18,000. Once known as Casa Fornaro, on account of its many bakeries, it still specialises in bread and various kinds of pasta. Other important manufacturing businesses include confectionery, soft drinks and furniture. The old quarter of winding streets and alleys lies to the north of the now much expanded town and the large number of sixteenth-century houses with elaborate balconies attests to its former importance. Here is the church of **St George** which is one of Malta's earliest grandiose buildings believed to be the work of Vittorio Cassar. Its tall façade and dominating front towers are symmetrically balanced by an ornate dome attributed to Gafà.

Beyond Qormi the route continues towards Żebbug, passing on the right negotiable country tracks leading to another of the island's many solitary churches. Surrounded by meticulously tended fields, this attractively situated sanctuary of **Tal Hlas** was designed by Gafà and dates from 1690. On the outskirts of Żebbug the road divides, the branch to the north-west crossing farmlands to meet the Attard-Mdina road (see page 129), the other turning southwards to Siġġiewi. Malta's main roads have a habit of skirting old *casal* centres and those by-passing Żebbug are no exceptions. But it would be difficult to miss this prominent hilltop town (population 9,950), bounded to the south-east by the steep slopes of Wied Baqqija.

ŻEBBUG

Formerly known as Città Rohan, the approach to **Żebbug's** centre is marked by the De Rohan Arch or Gate, erected in honour of Malta's penultimate Grand Master, Emmanuel de Rohan-Polduc (1775–97). Regarded as one of the Order's most learned and enlightened rulers, he worked to modernise the knightly image at a time when revolutionary fervour was sweeping his native France and European aristocracy and chivalrous affectations were increasingly seen as anachronistic. Neither de Rohan, nor least his successor Hompesch could save the Order, yet the reforms known as 'Code Rohan' survive as part of Maltese common law.

The Maltese name, Żebbug, refers to the large and profitable olive groves that once clothed this neighbourhood, only remnants of which survive. But the *casal* was also famous for its heavy sail cloth, manufactured from locally-grown cotton and exported all over Europe. The town's narrow streets with many old residences focus on the parish church of **St Peter** (1599) whose splendid front façade includes two ornate belfreys framing a graceful lantern dome set on an octagonal drum. Its rich interior includes a finely decorated coffered vault. Żebugg has a number of other early churches including the simply-styled **St Roque** (1593) whose diminutive forecourt once acted as a place of asylum.

Żebbug, for its size, has produced a surprising number of

Maltese notables, not least the patriots and national heroes Dun Mikiel Xerri and Mgr F X Caruana who were actively involved in the revolt against the French, the latter becoming the first Bishop of Malta under British rule. Other famous sons are the poet Dun Karm Psaila, the language scholar Mikiel Anton Vassalli and the sculptor Antonio Sciortino whose works can be seen in many parts of the islands.

SIĠĠIEWI

Southwards from Żebbug the main road to Siġġiewi crosses **Wied Qirda** and a narrow track on the right leads to the church of the Visitation where footpaths continue along this attractively rugged and invariably dry valley. Bounded by this *wied*, to the north-west and **Wied Xhora** to the south-east, **Siġġiewi** is another agriculturally productive hilltop settlement. Not to be outdone by the fame of neighbouring Żebbug, Siġġiewi was earlier named Città Fernandino (after the last of the Grand Masters) and it, too, is the birthplace of a number of Maltese notables such as the poets Karmenu Vassallo and Patri G Delia.

Visitors should not miss **Gafà's** parish church of St Nicholas of Bari built between 1675 and 1693, for it is one of Malta's finest Baroque buildings, its richly adorned interior containing Preti's last, unfinished painting. Other noteworthy buildings are the early eighteenth-century chapel of St Margaret and the seventeenth-century house of the Order's Inquisitorial Secretary, readily identified by its beautifully proportioned loggia. The Inquisitor himself had a summer palace in the hills to the south-west (see page 140), reached by a turning off the main Siġġiewi–Mdina road.

GHAR LAPSI

Southwards from Siġġiewi the road crosses the farmed areas known as **Tal-Lewza** and **Tal-Providenza**, the latter also being the name of a rural church seen on the left. Crossing the site of an old airfield the road descends a *wied*, first skirting the coastal inlet of **Ix-Xaqqa** before turning south-eastwards to **Għar Lapsi**. Meaning 'Cave of the Ascension' this small fishing and bathing cove has eating places, picnic areas and bus connections with Siġġiewi. There are excellent views across to the islet of Fifla, and from Għar Larsi coastal paths (somewhat strenuous) lead eastwards to the Blue Grotto area (see page 125).

4: North–Central Malta

Route 5 : Hamrun – Birkirkara – Attard – Lija – Mosta – Victoria Lines – Naxxar – Għargħur

Out of Valletta–Floriana, the routes to north-central Malta first pass through Hamrun and continue north-westwards either through Attard or Birkirkara where a series of main roads fan out to the towns and villages lying to the south-east of the Victoria Lines. The Hamrun–Attard road is also the main link between Valletta and Rabat–Mdina (see Route 6), though there are many and often less congested alternatives.

HAMRUN

This busy manufacturing and commercial section of the Valletta conurbation is usually choked with traffic, much of it funnelled along the town's high street. The Maltese anticipate delays and visitors heading west are provided ample stationary opportunities to share the frustrations of Malta's increasingly commuter-centralised society. To moribund passengers in Hamrun's main street of banks, shops, insurance offices and warehouses, the parish church of **St Cajeton** provides an important element of architectural variety. This nineteenth-century construction successfully blends the tenets of classical and Gothic style, but its main feature, a silver dome with close-spaced stone ribs was completed by Guzé Damato in 1958.

To the immediate north of Hamrun is **Blata l'Bajda**, a new residential town which is also the main accommodation centre for students of Malta University. Immediately west, in **Santa Venera**, are eighteenth-century villas with large gardens, though their former isolation is now stifled by urban sprawl. One such mansion is the Casa Leoni built in 1730 for Grand Master Manuel de Vilhena.

BIRKIRKARA

This elongated urban spread (population 18,000) is another of the conurbation's commercial and manufacturing towns with a modern industrial estate at San Gwann. Its old centre, however, is traditional Maltese with a pleasing mixture of simple one-storeyed homes and some large balconied mansions crowded into narrow winding streets. **St Helen's**, the parish church, was built by Domenico Cachia in 1735–45 and it is both one of the island's biggest and most beautiful, containing many valuable paintings and sacred treasures.

Joined to Birkirkara are Balzan, Lija and Attard, the latter more directly reached from Hamrun by the road which follows the ruined aqueduct built under the grand mastership of Alof de Wignacourt (1601–22) to provide Valletta with a more reliable water supply from the west. This route also parallels the old railway built by the British between Valletta and Mdina. Before Attard a road to the right passes under one of the line's old arches and then crosses the barely recognisable track of this once important communications link.

ATTARD

Effectively marking the western edge of the Valletta conurbation, this wealthy residential suburb has long been a place of prestigious villas and many are still surrounded by extensive gardens and citrus groves. The latter are the remnants of a once major orange-growing district prior to the competitive demands for suburban building land. As befitting Attard's obvious prosperity the church of **St Mary** has a richly carved façade and is considered to be the best work of Tommaso Dingli. It was built in 1613 when the architect was only 22 years old.

Attard's social prestige is currently maintained by the **San Anton Palace**, once the home of Grand Masters and British Governors but now Malta's official Presidential Residence. Disliking the isolation of the Verdala Palace (see page 140), which was a lengthy carriage ride from Valletta, Grand Master Antoine de Paule (1623–35) commissioned the enlargement of his private country home into the sumptuous palace that survives today, this, together with other extravagances, gave him the reputation of elderly self-indulgence and a love of sensuality and luxury – all of which greatly displeased the Inquisitor. The Order's disregard of frugality is said to have firmly begun under de Paule, his massive household descending in hierarchical order to include those who wound clocks, caught rats and baked black bread for his hunting dogs.

The bougainvillea – and ivy-clad palace is closed to visitors, but not its formal gardens which have many rare trees and other exotic plants, flower gardens and a small zoo. It is popular with Maltese and visitors of all ages and is a main stopping point on many organised excursions.

LIJA AND BALZAN

The **San Anton Gardens** act as the focal point of what are locally known as the Three Villages – **Attard**, **Lija** and

Balzan – and visitors might well find themselves entering from one settlement and leaving by a gate into another. Officially San Anton is part of **Balzan** where there are other large villas most of them presenting austere stone fronts to the streets. Citrus groves survive in many places and other available land is devoted to market gardening, specialising in flowers, soft fruits and salad vegetables. Balzan has many interesting churches, its main square dominated by the Baroque façade of the church of Annunciation (1669–95).

More old mansions with spacious gardens are found in **Lija** which adjoins Balzan to the north-west. Built by Giovanni Barbara in 1694, the somewhat austere parish church of St Saviour is more than brightened by its ornate interior.

MOSTA

From the Three Villages a choice of routes lead to **Mosta** whose name derives from an Arabic word meaning 'central', this large village (or town) lying close to the geographical centre of Malta. Not the most attractive of island settlements – for straight avenues have replaced many of its once sinuous streets – Mosta is mainly visited for its parish church of **St Mary** whose magnificent rotunda is Europe's third largest unsupported ecclesiastical dome, ranking after St Peter's in Rome and Istanbul's Santa Sophia.

Built in 1833–63 in imitation of the Roman Pantheon, its architect was Giorgio Groghet de Vassé, much of the labour being voluntary and most of the money raised by parishioners. The dome, spanning a diameter of nearly 123 feet, was constructed without the use of scaffolding and its enormity – a landmark throughout a large section of the island – is even better appreciated from inside, its optically spiralling pattern appearing to surge upwards into the sky. It is said that a standing congregation in excess of 10,000 can be accommodated in the main circular body of the church which also contains six side chapels amongst whose treasures are paintings by Cali and other Maltese artists.

Traditionally classical in style, St Mary's exterior façade is a forest of Ionic columns flanked by a pair of beautifully decorated bell-towers. The stone has weathered to a deep apricot hue and is an even more magnificent sight when illuminated for religious feasts, a major festival being that of the Assumption on 15 August. On this and other occasions its brilliantly illuminated interior highlights the splendour of its riches – precious metalled and jewelled votives, invaluable paintings and richly woven damasks. At all times a visit to St Mary's is an unforgettable experience.

Viewed from Mdina's battlements, the massive dome of Mosta's church dominates the scene from the citadel to the sea

The church has a small museum whose main exhibit is a large (now defused) German bomb which at 4.40 pm on 9 April 1942, dropped through the dome and landed on the floor during a church service attended by some 300 worshippers. No one was injured and, naturally, the people of Mosta annually celebrate this miracle.

THE VICTORIA LINES

Mosta is a good starting point for walks along the **Victoria Lines** and much of this scarp area, caused by the Great

Fault (see page 45), is also negotiable by car. The more elevated and sparsely settled south-western section is reached via the main Mosta–Żebbieh road where, at **Falka Gap**, a minor route follows the crest of the **Dwejra Ridge** (210 m) which offers extensive views in all directions. Close to **Binġemma Gap** are catacombs and the remains of prehistoric temples, beyond which the road rises to a further vantage point at the **Nadur Tower** (242 m). This section of the Lines can also easily be reached from Rabat–Mdina, prominently seen to the south-east.

The north-eastern section of the Lines can be visited by first taking the road out of Mosta to the roundabout at **Tarġa Gap**. It crosses the ruggedly attractive **Wied ta l'Isperanza** whose valley sides are the sites of ancient remains, catacombs, old churches and fortifications. Here there are impressive views of Malta's north-east coast as the road skirts the edge of the scarp to the **Naxxar Gap** and the village of Għargħur. Beyond, it circuitously drops down to the island's coastal road from the St Julian's area (see page 143) to Marfa.

NAXXAR AND GĦARGĦUR

Mainly agricultural and joined to Mosta, **Naxxar** has recently expanded as a residential village and has gained considerable importance as the venue for the Malta International Trade Fair, held in the grounds of Palazzo Parisio. According to tradition it was one of the first Maltese villages to fully accept Christianity, its parish church of Our Lady of Victories (1616) being another of Dingli's works. At **San Pawl tat-Targa** (adjoining Naxxar to the north) is the seventeenth-century church of St Paul close to the **Gauci Tower**, one of the main look-out points built by the Knights along this ridge. From Naxxar roads diverge in all directions, the one using the Naxxar Gap leading to Salina and St Paul's Bays.

Providing some of the best views, the smaller hilltop village of **Għargħur** boasts four seventeenth-century churches, including Dingli's St Bartholomew (1636). Within walking distance is the **Madliena Fort** built to protect the eastern coastal flank of the Victoria Lines.

5: Rabat–Mdina and the Dingli Heights

Route 6: Ta'Qali – Mdina – Rabat – Verdala – Buskett – Dingli

Throughout central Malta all roads lead to Rabat–Mdina,

the main route from Attard passing close to the impressive National Stadium and the **Ta'Qali Craft Village** which occupies the site of a World War II aerodrome. Here visitors can see artisans at work and purchase items direct from the producer at prices often cheaper than in the Valletta and Sliema souvenir shops. A great choice of handicrafts is available, including ceramics (vases, dishes, pots and decorative pieces), knitted garments, lace fabrics, wrought iron ware, filigree and other jewellery and glassware. The glass factories, with hand-blowing displays are extremely popular and produce an astonishing range of colourful items. The blend of turquoise and dark green is particularly attractive and there are other marble-effect colour combinations in browns. Other souvenirs are ornamental brass door-knockers, the dolphin variety seen on doors throughout the islands.

MDINA

The honey-coloured city of **Mdina** sits proudly on a hilltop and is one of Malta's most beautiful sights and main tourist attractions. At a height of some 200 metres, its citadel contains a near perfect medieval town, the dome and towers of its magnificent cathedral providing a major island landmark, especially when floodlit at night. From Mdina's battlements visitors are treated to a series of extensive views over the Maltese countryside, this eminence stressing its former role as a fortress and administrative capital. The main phases of its lengthy history have already been referred to and the various names by which it has been known reflect much of its character. The Arab name Mdina (Medina) implied *the* city, *par excellence*, and in the early fifteenth century Alfonso V of Aragon dubbed it *Città Notabile*. To distinguish it from their new urban creation, Valletta, the Knights referred to it as *Città Vecchia* ('Old City'). Now it is often called 'the Silent City' for an air of solitude and secretiveness, tinged with an element of intrigue, pervades its narrow historical streets. The description '*notabile*', however, still applies for many of the stately homes and palaces remain the properties of aristocratic families.

Mdina is usually entered by the narrow monumental bridge over a dry moat which divided the citadel (as it still does) from Rabat. Tunnelling under it is the old railway line from Valletta which led to the station to the north-west of the enceinte. The early eighteenth-century **Main** or **Mdina Gate** bears the arms of Grand Master Manoel de Vilhena (1722–36) and within the walls, to the right, is the

Magisterial or **Vilhena Palace**, designed by Giovanni Barbara. This now houses Malta's **Natural History Museum** with an especially interesting display dealing with the geological structure of the islands. On the opposite side of what is called St Publius Square (really a wide street) is the sixteenth-century **Torre dello Standardo**, the old gatehouse used today as a police headquarters.

St Publius Square leads to Inguanez Street off which is Mdina's main thoroughfare, **Villegaignon Street**, named after the Knight who organised the city's defence against the Turks in 1551. Close to this junction are the churches of St Benedict and St Agatha, the convent of St Benedict and **Casa Inguanez**, the palace home of Malta's oldest titled family. The modern looking façade belies its antiquity, but its ornate doorway in Mesquita Street indicates noble

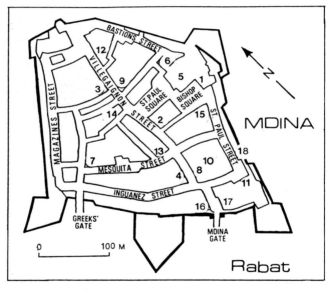

Street plan of Mdina

1. Archbishop's Palace
2. Banca Giuratale
3. Carmelite Church
4. Casa Inguanez
5. Cathedral
6. Cathedral Museum
7. Chapel of St Nicholas
8. Church of St Peter
9. Church of St Roque
10. Convent of St Benedict
11. Corte Capitanale
12. Norman House (Palazzo Falzon)
13. Palazzo Gatto-Murina
14. Palazzo Santa Sophia
15. Seminary (Museum)
16. Tower of the Standard (Police Station)
17. Magisterial Palace (Museum)
18. Xara Palace

The main gate into Mdina, Malta's historical and architectural treasure house

occupancy. Though secretively closed to the streets, visitors will recognise other aristocratic mansions by the quality of their entrance architecture, not least **Gatto-Murina** which is also in Mesquita Street.

Halfway along Villegaignon Street is **St Paul's Square** leading to Mdina's co-cathedral, its bishopric duties shared with St John's in Valletta. Reputed to stand on the site of Publius's house when St Paul landed on Malta, this Baroque masterpiece built to the plan of a Latin cross is the work of Gafà who replaced an earlier cathedral destroyed by earthquake in 1693. Built in 1697–1702, **St Paul's** is somewhat less ornate than other Maltese grand churches, but its dignified front façade with three pilastered entrances is topped by beautifully proportioned bell-towers. The dome, its crowning glory, is best seen from other parts of the city and environs. Guarding the main door are a pair of Maltese cannon that spent some time on display in Woolwich Artillery Museum before returning to Mdina in 1888.

A detail of the rich interior splendour of Mdina's co-cathedral dedicated to St Paul

The interior of St Paul's vies with St John's in Valletta as providing Malta's most glorious ecclesiastical experience, for it presents a magnificent display of artistic craftsmanship blending the qualities of stone, wood, paint, glass, precious metals and fabrics. Tour guides stop at Mattia Preti's lively mural of *The Shipwreck of St Paul* and their charges are directed to other highlights, including the large silver and gilt cross said to have been carried by Godfrey de Bouillon on the First Crusade and brought to Malta from Rhodes by the Knights. But the main church and its side chapels offer much more, and their exhibits carry informative explanations and descriptions for the independent visitor.

To the left of the cathedral's entrance the **Museum**, housed in an old seminary, contains many relics saved from the earlier church, together with modest displays of Punic and Roman artefacts. It also has a valuable display of paintings and engravings by many famous European artists and of great interest are the beautifully illuminated choirbooks dating from the eleventh century. The fascinating coin collections summarise the history and past rulers of the islands.

An ornate palazzo doorway in Mdina's St Paul's Square

Back to Villegaignon Street, a short walk past other old palaces leads to **Bastion Street** and **Square** at the north-west corner of Mdina's battlements. Here there are magnificent views over the Maltese countryside and with the help of a good map the villages, large churches and topographical features can easily be named and located.

Returning to Main Gate, visitors should explore the quarters to the west of Villegaignon Street where narrow streets and alleys, some no wider than an outstretched arm, are full of visual surprises. Particularly pleasing is the decorative detail of the domestic architecture – fine window mouldings, armorial reliefs, ornate doors and knockers, wayside shrines and a variety of wrought iron street lamps. But some Mdina streets are sombre, especially **St Paul's Street** which, from the cathedral, parallels the eastern ramparts. It leads to a small square and the **Xara Palace Hotel,** formerly the home of another aristocratic family and for the price of a refreshment visitors can gain some idea of the character of a once noble home. The figures of Mercy and Justice on the building facing the hotel indicate its earlier function as **Mdina's Court of Law,** and the square's graceful loggia was the place where the city herald proclaimed news and, often, laws and edicts.

RABAT

The name of this busy market town for the western part of the island means 'suburb' for it grew as an extension of Mdina, particularly during Roman times when the entire settlement was referred to as Melita. It was the Arabs who reduced its compass to the area of Mdina's present citadel, the rest of the town declining and falling into disrepair. Rabat's rejuvenation was a consequence of more settled times under the Knights and the British and today the 'suburb' has far surpassed in size the mother town which spawned it. Untidy modern growth belies its former importance and it contains many venues of historical interest. Collectively, Rabat–Mdina provide the inquisitive tourist with more than enough to fill a full day's sightseeing.

On leaving Mdina's Main Gate, a sweep of shrubs, trees and flowerbeds form Howard Gardens which merge with the main bus terminus and the large coach and car park serving Rabat–Mdina. To the south, Museum Road leads to the columned **Roman Villa,** a modern building over the remains of what was obviously a rich Roman town house. Its ground floor has a large collection of Greek, Punic and Roman artefacts from local discoveries and other parts of Malta. One display is devoted to oil lamps, many of them carrying the fish and cross motifs used in Christian catacombs. Downstairs the atmosphere is truly Roman for this old atrium area, now lined with busts and columns, is centred around a number of mosaic floors unearthed in 1881, one of the most famous depicting two naiads molesting a satyr – an artistic piece of antique mugging!

From the Museum Esplanade, St Paul's Street leads to the centre of Rabat and **Parish Square** where the richly ornate **Church of St Paul** stands. Much of its present form, probably the work of Gafà (notably the dome) is late seventeenth century when remodelling combined elements of an earlier church containing a chapel of Publius. Beneath the church is a much venerated cave or grotto, reputed to be the 'dwelling' or 'prison' of St Paul. The seventeenth-century statue of the apostle was presented by Grand Master Pinto. The grotto is steeped with legend, one story relating that no matter how much stone is extracted, the cave remains the same size.

Rabat's irregular streets are punctuated by other interesting churches, including **Ta Doni** and **Ta Gesù** (St Paul's Street) and **St Augustine** (St Augustine Street), this being Gerolamo Cassar's first important church. Built in 1571, it has a Renaissance-style façade with rose window and a massive barrel vaulted interior, a forerunner to his work on St John's, Valletta. In an amorphous-shaped square close to St Paul's is the small chapel of **St Cataldus** which visitors will pass on the way to **St Paul's** and **St Agatha's Catacombs** reached from St Agatha's Street. Both are extensive underground systems of maze-like galleries, alcoves and passageways cut out of the rock face at various levels. They were used as fourth–fifth century burial places and include numerous loculi or horizontal recesses, canopied table graves and saddleback tombs imitating classical sarcophagi. A characteristic feature of Maltese catacombs are the round 'agape tables' cut from the rock with slanting sides. Here mourners reclined to partake of farewell meals. Other Roman catacombs of interest are those of **Abbatija tad-Dejr** in Rabat's Bir ir-Riebu district.

Rabat is a good centre for touring many parts of the island, but especially Malta's area of highest land referred to as the Dingli Heights or Plateau (see page 45). The town's bus terminus at Saqqajja Square is the focus of a number of island roads and an easy excursion can be made to the Buskett and Dingli areas by first following Buskett Road. On the town's southern edge it diverges, one branch leading past the Verdala Palace to Buskett and on to the cliffs, the other heading directly to Dingli where it also continues to the coast, following the wild land edge to join the road from Buskett.

A circuit tour can also be made by using the inland link between Dingli and Buskett, and many minor roads, leading back to Rabat, to explore further this intriguing area.

THE VERDALA PALACE

After Rabat, the fir-lined road crosses open country, passing windmills used for irrigation. A turn-off to the left is the main approach to **Verdala Palace** prominently situated on a hill. Designed by Gerolamo Cassar in 1586 as a summer home for Grand Master Huges de Loubenx Verdalle (1581–95), the structure is that of a square fortified medieval castle complete with moat. The latter is recorded as being the scene of many a suicide during Verdalle's tyrannical office, his servants and slaves preferring to take their own lives rather than suffer torture for what were minor actions that displeased him. Beneath the palace are dungeons where his victims were chained and these also housed French prisoners in the early nineteenth century.

Verdala now plays host to official guests of the Maltese government and is not usually open to the public, though visitors should check with tourist offices. Its long driveway leads through a parkland of cypresses, carobs, pines and orange groves which form part of Buskett Gardens, also referred to as Boschetto ('Little Wood').

BUSKETT GARDENS

As noted, **Buskett** is the venue for the traditional Imnarja Festival, but the gardens are a favourite retreat of Maltese and visitors throughout much of the year. Their origin as a recreational area preceded the building of Verdala, the Knights reafforesting this area and laying it out with game enclosures. Though animals of the chase were few, Malta proved to be a good island for hawking and the fame of the Maltese falcon has taken its place in history.

Buskett vies as being one of the most attractive parts of the island, its footpaths making it an ideal place for exploratory walks. The more strenuous can head for the **Inquisitors Summer Palace** (built in 1625 for Honoratus Visconti) on the slopes of **Wied Girgenti**. The Inquisition, the papal instrument for the suppression of heresy, was established in Malta in 1542, and this beautifully proportioned palace in an attractive setting was obviously a good place to escape from heavy official duties. Recently renovated, it is not open to the public but there are plans to turn it into a museum. Further paths eastwards lead to **Tas-Salib** Hill (218 metres), also known as **Laferla Cross** with its crowning church of the Annunciation. This part of the island is also easily reached from Siġġiewi.

DINGLI AND ITS CLIFFS

The village of **Dingli** has at least two claims to fame, being the birthplace of the famous architect after whom it is named and also being Malta's highest village. It is further noted for its irrigated fields and orchards and has long been a centre of productive agriculture. From the village there is access to many parts of its high cliffs where this edge of Malta drops some 250 precipitous metres to the sea. Perched on the very edge of this shore is the chapel of St Mary Magdalene (1646), undoubtedly one of Malta's loneliest sanctuaries.

6. *North-Western Malta*

Rabat-Mdina, Mosta and Naxxar are important gateways to this area of rugged ridges and fertile, flat-bottomed valleys (see page 45) beyond the Victoria Lines. As noted, the north-west was less settled in the past and has comparatively few villages. Nowadays, however, tourism has changed many sections of its coastline, especially around St Paul's and Mellieħa Bays. The entire coastline is one of rugged headlands separated by large bays and ancillary coves, and many of these are popular resort areas.

From City Gate two main bus routes (via Mosta) serve the northwseset, one to Żebbieħ, Mġarr and Għajn Tuffieħa, and the other to St Paul's Bay, Mellieħa and Marfa-Ċirkewwa. An attractive alternative for visitors with their own transport is the St Julian's–St Paul's Bay coastal route which, joining the buses out of Valletta, continues on to Marfa. Other main and country roads serve the north-west, many of them guided by the ridge and valley topography and usefully linking this part of the island's opposite shores.

Route 7: *Mosta – Żebbieh – Għajn Tuffieħa – Mġarr*

From Mosta, via the Falka Gap through the Victoria Lines, this route heads north-westwards across fertile farmlands to the small and unassuming village of **Żebbieħ**, chiefly a stop-over for those visiting the **Skorba Temple** remains (see page 62). Żebbieħ, as such, is hardly mentioned in guidebooks for it has few buildings of monumental signifi-cance, yet its cubic-style domestic architecture has much appeal, the village retaining an atmosphere of times past when this part of the island was lightly defended. The economy is essentially farming-based and the highlights of Żebbieh's day seem to be the bus arrivals from Valletta. The village is a junction for roads leading to the bays at Għajn Tuffieħa and, via Mġarr, Ġnejna.

GHAJN TUFFIEHA

The road from Żebbieh skirts the western edge of the Wardija Ridge where it joins the route from St Paul's Bay to Għajn Tuffieħa. Before this junction are the remains of Roman steam baths complete with antique public lavatories, the site restored with UNESCO funds in 1961. Reaching the coast, a headland with look-out tower separates **Golden Bay** to the north from **Għajn Tuffieħa Bay** to the south, both being popular sandy beaches with hotels.

MĠARR

Within walking distance of Żebbieh, **Mġarr** is a larger farming village also basically unchanged except for its huge ovoid-domed **Church of the Assumption**, a modern edifice built from local donations. The dome's unusual shape is explained by the fact that its funding came mainly from the sale of village eggs. A small tight nucleus of narrow alleyways huddle around this grand fabric, the rest of the village following an unfinished grid-iron plan which is the product of later growth. At the village's eastern entrance are the **Ta'Hagrat temple** remains which are similarly dated to those of Skorba.

To the west of Mġarr is the aristocratic home of the Cassia family – the **Zammitello Palace** – which occupies an eminence to the left of where the road drops into the Ġnejna Valley, reaching the coast in the sandy **Ġnejna Bay** with its look-out tower. This is the start (or end) of a popular

Haġar Qim, a temple dating from the Third Millenium BC

walk between Ġnejna Bay and Rabat, a rough distance of
12.5 kilometres. Crossing the neck of Ras il-Pellegrin, it
follows the steep cliff face above **Fomm ir-Riħ Bay** where
a minor road to the south-west passes Kuncizzioi Church
(back within the Victoria Lines) and continues on to Rabat.

Route 8: St Julian's – Salina Bay – St Paul's Bay – Mellieħa – Marfa

Leaving St Julian's through Paceville (see page 114), this
road first passes the old barrack areas of the British
occupation, those of St Andrew's merging with Pembroke
Fort and reaching the coast at St George's. This extensive
military area has now been adapted to Maltese civil uses,
especially residential. Here the Victoria Lines are in close
proximity of Greater Valletta and passing Madliena Fort on
the right, the road descends beyond their limit to the shore
reaching the large recreational complex and children's fun
park at Baħar iċ-Ċagħaq Bay.

SALINA BAY

Crossing the base of Qrejten Point with its old watchtower
the road hugs the rocky coast to Għallis Point with another
of the Knight's defensive structures. It stands at the eastern
entrance to **Salina Bay** named after its extensive saltpans,
this industry being a lucrative monopoly of the Knights. At
the head of the bay is the **Kennedy Memorial Grove**
designed in 1966 to commemorate the assassinated Ameri-
can president. Continuing in the direction of San Pawl il-
Baħar (St Paul's Bay) a junction leads north to encircle the
Qawra peninsula which bounds Salina Bay to the west, its
coastline now largely built-up. Rounding its head at the
Qawra Tower, another look-out defence, it reaches
Buġibba, Malta's fastest growing tourist area with some of
the island's most up-to-date amenities and a 'costa'
atmosphere.

ST PAUL'S BAY

Qawra Point provides excellent views across St Paul's Bay to
St Paul's Islands (little more than rocks) where the apostle's
ship is said to have grounded. A scientific project is
currently investigating this area in the hope of substantiat-
ing the New Testament account. On the larger islet, called
Selmunett in Maltese, is a statue of St Paul (erected in
1845) and on feast days it is the site of open-air masses.
  Buġibba merges with **San Pawl il-Baħar** close to where

the Wignacourt Tower guards the old fishing harbour – **Rdum l-Abjad** – and its surviving old houses. Close by is St Paul's Church, the traditional spot of the famous snake-bite incident (see page 69). Beyond, at the innermost part of the main bay, is **Għajn Rasul** (Apostle's Fountain) where Paul is said to have struck a rock which miraculously brought forth a gushing spring. Perhaps this was not so wonderful, for the verdant Pwales Valley leading south-westwards is naturally fed from underground springs which accounts for its year-round profitable crops. A useful main road from St Paul's to Għajn Tuffieħa follows the edge of **Wardija Ridge** which provides attractive countryside walks.

MELLIEĦA

From St Paul's Bay the Mellieħa road passes through **Xemxija**, a further extension of the tourism zone. Sinu-ously climbing the **Bajda Ridge**, the road drops into the Mistra Valley where a side road to the right follows the rugged Kalkara Ravine to **Mistra Bay**, a small appendage to St Paul's. A rough track up to an old battery provides marvellous coastal views. Back on the main road the steep slopes of **Mellieħa Ridge** are negotiated, a side road leading to the **Selmun Palace**, built in 1789 to the design of Domenico Cachia, its fortress style resembling the Verdala Palace.

Standing at the centre of the ridge which bears its name, **Mellieħa** (population 5,000) is another of Malta's dominat-ing villages. Abandoned in the sixteenth century, its street pattern takes the form of a gridiron structure, for it is largely a planned village of the nineteenth century when the north-west was actively recolonised. Below the impressively sited parish church of **Our Lady of Victory** is a venerated grotto with a miraculous spring. It contains a faded fresco of the Virgin which is attributed to St Luke who was shipwrecked with St Paul.

Acting as the unofficial capital of the north, Mellieħa is a busy marketing centre. Its northern edge clings to the ridge's craggy slopes, deeply cut by short valleys leading to the southern coast of the wide Mellieħa Bay. The ridge itself is another area for scenic walks.

Skirting the sandy edge of **Mellieħa Bay**, popular with water sports enthusiasts and another tourism growth area, the road now reaches the north-western extremities of Malta. It climbs the last of the ridges – **Marfa Ridge** – where there are superb views across to Comino and Gozo. On the left is the **Torri l-Aħmar** or Red Tower (1649), once guardian of this important route. Descending to the coast, a series of straight routes afford access from the main ridge road to the north's popular bays. Much traffic, however, heads for **Marfa Point** (Ċirkewwa), the landing stage for the 20-minute ferry journey to Gozo which passes close to the south-west coast of Comino.

The Ċirkewwa-Gozo ferry arriving from Mġarr

TOURING GOZO

**Mġarr – Xewkija – Victoria – Sannat – Xlendi –
Għarb and Ta'Pinu – San Lawrenz and Dwerja –
Żebbuġ and Marsalforn – Xagħra and Ramla Bay
– Nadur and Qala**

Gozo is not a miniature Malta, but an island with its own
personality. Not only do visitors recognise this, but also the
Maltese. As noted, it differs from its larger sister island both
in physical appearance and in the character of its people –
some would argue their ethnic appearance as well. There
are, of course, many similarities, for from prehistoric times
onwards Gozo's history has been tied to that of Malta's. Yet
less defended Gozo and a land apart from Malta, made it an
easier prey to Mediterranean marauders, the islanders
consequently suffering more adversity. Frequently they fell
victim to Moslem raids when whole villages were destroyed
and their inhabitants carried off in captivity. When highly
defended Malta successfully rebuffed the Ottoman navy
Gozo had already been sacked by the Turks, its able-bodied
deported to slave markets, chiefly those of Constantinople.
Not surprisingly periods of devastation and poverty bred,
on the part of the islanders, a wariness of strangers and
intruders and it has been suggested that on at least one
occasion the population was so depleted that immigration
from Sicily was needed to replace it. According to some
scholars this accounts for the differing physical appearance
of the Gozitans though, at the same time, the rape of their
island led to outwith migration, in more recent times mainly
to the USA, Canada and Australia. Many have subsequently returned to enhance the modern reconstruction not
only of their native island but of Malta as a whole. A
considerable amount of foreign-earned capital has gone into
Gozo's developing tourism infrastructure.

In the words of Quentin Hughes (see page 166) '. . . Gozo
traditionally feels that it is badly done by. This is England's
Wales, Italy's Sicily, the less fortunate province, and yet it is
this very isolation and its partial neglect by the Knights and
the British, who had little need for an island without good
harbours, that has left it in a more primitive state, less
damaged by unsuitable development'. Compared to Malta,
Gozo's tourist commercialisation is a recent addition to the

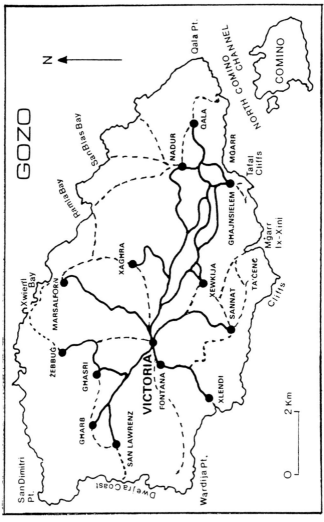

island's economy and there are many who feel, islanders and visitors, that the spate of recent development should be curbed at its current level. Gozo, they argue, still retains elements of peace, serenity and old-style authenticity, and the tragedy would be if this atmosphere was progressively eroded. But the problem is the island itself, for its alluring landscapes and, despite their past troubles, the friendly and hospitable Gozitans, together cast a spell over visitors who spend time getting to know it. Gozo has a tradition of enchantment and the islanders embellish the story of it being the ancient Ogygia where Homer's shipwrecked

Odysseus fell under the wily charms of Calypso who enticed him to stay for seven years. Though there are many Mediterranean claimants for the authentic (if at all) location of Ogygia, the appeal of Gozo, marketed as 'Calypso's Isle', is such that it seduces back many holidaymakers. Others opt to stay for more than seven years by buying island homes!

Even more than Malta, this is a centralised island with all the main roads and bus routes leading out of the capital, Victoria. Public transport, however, is more restricted, and those with private cars will find themselves returning to Victoria for there are few circuit routes. Gozo's main settlements are located inland as a former security against piracy, and the prominent table-like hill sites of most main villages offered further protection. Yet hardly any part of the island is out of reach of the good walker.

MĠARR

Gozo's busiest road is that covering the short distance between Victoria and **Mġarr**, the island's landfall from Malta. This port and attendant village offers a suitably scenic entry to the island, the stout breakwaters of its harbour containing a colourful assemblage of *luzzu* cargo and fishing boats, yachts and other pleasure craft and the busy ferries for Sa Maison Wharf and Ċirkewwa on Malta. The attractive waterside buildings provide all facilities for incoming passengers – post office, bank, tourist office, police station, small guest houses, snack bars, and souvenir shops. But there is still much to indicate that Mġarr remains an active fishing port.

Dominating the view, and a landmark for much of the journey from Malta is **Our Lady of Lourdes**, a nineteenth-century church designed by Emmanuel Galizia

Churches dominate the scene on arrival at Mġarr, Gozo

Gothic style is somewhat alien to the Baroque architectural traditions of the islands. To the south-west, occupying the top of Tafal Cliffs is **Fort Chambray**, designed in the eighteenth century as a defended township to control the Gozo–Malta passage, its cost defrayed by the French Knight Jacques François de Chambray. The town never fully materialised and the British used it as a barracks and hospital for their garrison on Gozo. Now partly used as a tourist complex it offers fine views over Mġarr Harbour and across to Comino and Malta.

XEWKIJA

It is only five kilometres from Mġarr to the outskirts of Victoria. The road climbs a steep *wied* through the contiguous village of **Għajnsielem** passing both a massive new church built on a prominent spur and the Knight's tower of Santa Cecilja which defended the Mġarr–Victoria road. Crossing the main road from Qala (see below), the village of **Xewkija** lies to the left, its massive church of St John the Baptist dominating this area and providing a readily recognisable landmark throughout much of Gozo. Built between 1952 and 1973 around the older parish church (which was later demolished) it is the work of Damato and was constructed largely by voluntary village labour and subscription. In true inter-island rivalry it was meant to surpass the dimensions of Mosta and its height, appearing more prominent from its elevated position, partly achieves this distinction, though the diameter of its dome is a number of metres smaller. Its style is Venetian Baroque, modelled on the Salute but with numerous variations that fully indicate Damato's architectural ingenuity.

From Xewkija, main island roads lead north to Xagħra, north-west to Nadur and Qala and south to Sannat. Continuing westwards Victoria is reached.

VICTORIA

The Gozitans still refer to their capital by the Arabic name **Rabat**, the modern town being the much enlarged suburb of the old citadel (Gran Castello), this being a similar, but smaller version of the Rabat–Mdina relationship on the main island. The British officially renamed it Victoria in honour of the Queen's diamond jubilee of 1887.

From Mġarr and Xewkija, Victoria (population 5,000) is entered along Racecourse Street (officially Republic Street), named after the traditional animal races associated with various festas. On the right is the entrance to **Rundle**

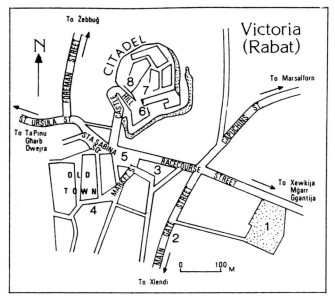

Street plan of Victoria

1. Rundle Gardens
2. Bus Terminus
3. Post Office
4. Church of St George
5. It-Tokk
6. Museum
7. Cathedral
8. Old Bishop's Palace

Gardens, an attractively landscaped park named after Sir Leslie Rundle, Governor of Malta, 1909–15. The setting for the evening *passaggiata*, Racecourse Street leads to **It-Tokk**, the shady main square which is continued as St George's Square. Archaeological work in this area has indicated that this might have been the old Roman forum, a function that continues today for It-Tokk (literally 'meeting place') is the scene of a busy morning market enticing both Gozitans and visitors. The square contains a number of important buildings, including the ornate bow-fronted **Banca Giuratale**, the old administrative centre built at the time of Grand Master Vilhena and now housing the Gozo information office. Here, too, is **St James Church** erected in 1740 on the site of an earlier building destroyed by the Turks. It contains a venerated statue of Our Lady of Sorrows. In its own square is the beautifully proportioned Baroque edifice of **St George's**, its front (1818) replacing that damaged by earthquake in 1693. The entire area to the south continues Victoria's old quarter, a picturesque section of narrow, animated streets and simple, but attractive houses.

North of It-Tokk, **Castle Hill** leads off Racecourse Street and steeply climbs to the old citadel, occupying the most central of Gozo's prominent flat-topped hills. The stout walls largely date from the sixteenth century onwards and at one time were capable of sheltering the entire population of the island. On entering the fortifications, visitors find themselves in an irregularly-shaped square almost entirely filled by a massive flight of cannon-guarded steps leading up to the west door of Rabat's **Cathedral**. The setting has to rank as one of the most beautiful architectural assemblages on the islands for the great church is flanked by other period buildings with ornate mouldings. The cathedral is not all-together what it seems for this western façade, though not apparent from this point, is built as a screen designed, it appears, for a much larger building. Its lavishly decorated interior reveals further signs of incompletion, for the dome was never constructed; instead the flat ceiling is painted in intricate perspective (the work of Antonio Manuele) to indicate what the presence of a towering central dome would have visually provided. This convincing *trompe l'oeil* is a masterful example of artistic illusionism. The church is also famous for the coloured mosaic tombs of past bishops and priests and it further houses a rich collection of paintings and precious ecclesiastical furniture.

The area around the cathedral houses Gozo's main museums. **The Cathedral Museum** at the back of the church has displays of ecclesiastical vestments, paintings and other religious decorations. Close by, in converted late medieval houses, is the **Folklore Museum** which exhibits farming and handicraft implements together with traditional costumes. The **Archaeological Museum** occupies a seventeenth-century house known as **Casa Bondi** and provides a detailed chronological array of prehistoric and historic artefacts found on Gozo. The cathedral area of the citadel has other interesting buildings, but unlike Mdina a large section within the walls is ruinous and overgrown. Walking its ramparts, however, visitors are treated to a series of panoramas covering most of the island. Here, too, the proportions of the unfinished cathedral can best be seen, particularly the massive bell-tower at its eastern end.

SANNAT

Located close to the coast to the south of Victoria and Xewkija, **Sannat** is Gozo's principal lace-making village. Lace is one of the island's longest established handicrafts, the work being extremely delicate and can be purchased as beautifully intricate doilies or as borders to handkerchiefs, tablecloths and other linen items. The northern and eastern approaches to the village are guarded by old knightly towers, but Sannat's proudest monument is the parish church of **St Margaret**, a fine piece of Baroque architecture built in 1718. Beyond the elongated spread of the village are the cliffs of **Ta'Ċenċ** with their steep, unscalable drop of 180 metres to the sea. They are the nesting places of many rare birds. East of the **Ta'Ċenċ Hotel** a track, leading past cart ruts, dolmens and other prehistoric remains drops into a rugged *wied* and the tiny inlet of **Mġarr ix-Xini**. Its small beach is surrounded by bare limestone cliffs and is one of the highlights of the coastal walk from Fort Chambray to Sannat.

Westwards from Sannat walkers can reach **Xlendi** by a number of tracks, the easiest route via the small settlement of **Munxar**. From Victoria Xlendi is quickly reached by a main south-west road, first passing through **Fontana** with its roadside wash-house of the Knights, dating to the seventeenth century. This unusual arch-roofed building is crowned by a statue of the Madonna and its cave-like interior is still used by villagers.

XLENDI

Still a fishing village, recent developments have turned **Xlendi** into one of the most sought after holiday places on Gozo. From Fontana it is approached through the steep Xlendi Valley, the village standing at the head of a bay protected by bare limestone headlands, those less steep colonised by modern holiday accommodation. In summer the narrow sandy beach is crowded, its clear water and that around the cave-etched promontories (accessible by boat) being excellent for swimming and snorkelling. The south-

The harbour front at Xlendi

ern entrance to the bay is guarded by **Xlendi Tower** (built in 1658), this area being the scene of much underwater archaeological research, the artefacts from early shipwrecks displayed in Victoria's Archaeological Museum.

Xlendi provides a range of accommodation and eating places, its souvenir shops offering a variety of local handicrafts, especially Gozo lace and visitors can watch its patient execution by local women.

GHARB AND TA'PINU

Just as Malta beyond the Victoria Lines was a 'frontier region', so western Gozo was even more prone to neglect and devastation, this part of the island being the last area to be safely settled and earning the title of 'the desert'. Despite this, its smaller villages boast some of the island's oldest and most authentic domestic architecture, not least **Għarb** where many homes are decorated with early stone-carved balconies, especially those surrounding the parish church of the Immaculate Conception. Quentin Hughes labels this as the most exciting Baroque church on Gozo for it has a flowery concave façade which features the sculptures depicting Faith, Hope and Charity. The symmetrical bell-towers are grafted on to earlier stumps which frame a rococo-style roofscape with equally flamboyant dome.

But the main landmark in this part of the island is the **Ta'Pinu Sanctuary** which dramatically rises from the Gozitan landscape on the road from Għarb to Għammar. This massive Neo-Romanesque structure with a separate and towering campanile was built in 1920–23 to replace a worn sixteenth-century chapel of Our Lady of the Assumption. Here, in 1883, the voice of the Virgin was heard by Carmela Grima, a woman of Għarb, and other acts of grace and miracles followed, including Gozo escaping the plague in the year following. Offerings were sent to the church from all over Malta and abroad, and these formed the funds for the modern construction which was raised to the papal dignity of a Basilica in 1932. Commemorating the name of Filippino Gauci (known as Pinu), Ta'Pinu is a twentieth-century example of skilled workmanship in Maltese stone. It is a national shrine and centre of pilgrimage for the whole of Malta. Formerly associated with the church, the set of life-size Carrara marble statues, representing the Stations of the Cross, have been erected along **Għammar Hill** overlooking the sanctuary.

Those intrigued by the Ta'Pinu miracles will want to visit the signposted home of Carmela Crima which is now a small museum.

SAN LAWRENZ AND DWERJA

Also in the Għarb area is the **Ta'Dbiegi Craft Village**, a much smaller version of Ta'Qali on Malta. The collection of purpose-built stone shops proffer a range of island handicrafts most of which are also available in It-Tokk and other island markets. Close by is San Lawrenz, a village with a similar atmosphere to Għarb and an elegant Baroque church with one of the most pleasing domes on Gozo. The writer Nicholas Monserrat lived and worked here until his death in 1979.

From San Lawrenz a road drops down to the Dwejra coast of western Gozo, an area of outstanding natural beauty. Across the entrance to the cave-riddled cliffs of **Dwejra Bay** (guarded by Qawra Tower) is **Fungus Rock**, the name being a misnomer for the growth covering it is a tiny shrub-like plant which the Arabs referred to as 'the treasure of drugs'. The Knights also harvested and jealously guarded this plant which they used as a dressing for wounds and a cure for dysentery. In 1744 Grand Master Pinto de Fonsca decreed it out of bounds for boats, and access, by authorised personnel only, was by means of a wicker basket suspended on a ropeway. Until the middle of the nineteenth century there was an official guardian of Fungus Rock.

A little to the north of Qawra Tower a small chapel stands vigil above what the Gozitans call **Il-Qawra** or the **Inland Sea**, a large eroded and cliff encircled limestone hollow forming a closed inland harbour whose only link with the sea is a scenic tunnel through the rock. Nearby is **It-Tiega** (**The Window**), an eroded archway in the coastal limestone and in imminent danger of collapse. The sea around Dwejra is intensely blue and provides some of the best snorkel swimming in the islands. In addition the cliff edges provide exhilarating walks but certain sections are dangerously rocky. Carved into the foreshore are numerous saltpans, this still actively pursued industry being one of the most ancient on Gozo.

ŻEBBUĠ AND MARSALFORN

This is a circuit trip which can be made from Victoria, first heading northwards to **Żebbuġ**, one of Gozo's highest villages. It occupies a steep ridge providing fabulous views over coast and countryside. Żebbuġ's church, consecrated in 1726, has the distinction of being the first on Gozo to be built with aisles. Its altar and other beautiful sculptures are carved from Gozo marble (or onyx) which has been quarried at Żebbuġ, though in limited quantities, since the early eighteenth century.

Noted for its handwoven woollen blankets and cotton cloth Żebbuġ, like many Gozitan villages, is long and straggling and to the south-west its houses merge with those of **Għasri**, another elevated settlement.

A lesser road steeply descends to the north coast at the small bathing inlet of **Xwieni Bay**. Along this part of the shore are Gozo's biggest saltpans which date from 1740. They consist of shallow trays cut into the limestone foreshore. In the winter months sea spray is blown across them and the summer sun evaporates this leaving a deposit of salt.

Negotiating a series of headlands **Marsalforn** is reached, Gozo's most popular holiday venue whose general character resembles that of Malta's Marsaxlokk. Though retaining much of its traditional fishing character (fresh fish is available in its restaurants throughout the year) it is now decidedly geared to tourism but is not spoilt by over-commercialisation. It has a small sandy beach, several hotels, guest houses, holiday flats, souvenir shops and other tourist amenities.

XAGHRA AND RAMLA BAY

Marsalforn is directly linked to Victoria by an attractive road which climbs through the fertile Marsalforn Valley, one of Gozo's most productive farming areas. A road also leads to **Xagħra**, a large nebula-shaped village which takes its form from the contours of the eroded plateau on which it stands. The Xagħra area is rich in archaeological remains, the main feature being the **Ġgantija Temple** remains regarded by many as being the most impressive of these

Rural landscape, Gozo

complexes on the islands. Excavated in 1827 it comprises of a main and subsidiary temple and a large forecourt, but most impressive are the massive stones which make up the perimeter wall. Visitors will certainly appreciate the name – Ġgantija – the legend being that a monstrous woman or group of giants built these temples. From the village they can be reached by Parisot Street or a path across the fields.

In the village are two caves of prehistoric interest, **Xerri's Grotto** and **Ninu's Grotto**. Both lie under private houses and have stalagmite and stalactite formations. In the main square is the parish church of **Our Lady of Victories**, the interior having wide aisles and massive columns inlaid with marble. Another of Xagħra's attractions is a stone-built windmill, one of a number built on Gozo during the time of Grand Master Maude de Vilhena.

North-east out of Xagħra a road descends intricately terraced slopes to **Ramla Bay**, the largest sandy beach on the islands and excellent for swimming. Overlooking the bay, close to a restaurant, is **Calypso's Cave** which itself offers little spectacle, but a visit to this Homeric spot is recommended for the beautiful view over the extensive beach with its red-tinted sands. At the bay's eastern end are submerged remains of a Roman villa, the western end having a redoubt erected by the Knights. Attractive walks are possible along the fretted coastline to **San Blas Bay** (see page 9) and beyond.

NADUR AND QALA

Nadur is an important route centre for the eastern part of Gozo with roads linking it to Victoria, Mġarr, Qala, Ramla Bay, San Blas Bay and other parts of the coast. Its main feature of interest is the monumental church of **St Peter and St Paul** which was erected on the site of a smaller building after Nadur became a parish in 1688, but the aisles, dome and front façade – more reminiscent of a government building than a church – are much later additions. With a long seafaring tradition Nadur is a wealthy town (second in size only to Victoria) and this is revealed by the church's interior which is awe-inspiringly rich to the point of ecclesiastical vulgarity. Nadur means 'summit' and its plateau-like position offers vantage points in all directions. The Knights kept a guard here at all times and from their **Kenuno Tower** were able to observe the whole of the island's east coast. The area around was another of Wignacourt's shooting preserves and many attractive gardens and wooded areas remain.

A main road eastwards leads to **Qala**, passing close to

another old windmill, the last to be worked on Gozo. Qala'a **Sanctuary of the Immaculate Conception** dates to the eleventh century, the present structure being the composite product of a series of subsequent enlargements. The village also commands extensive views and beyond the centre of the village the road curves round to Qala Cliffs above the tiny inlet of **Honoq ir-Rummien** with its minuscule sandy beach. The seascape is marvellous and offers an almost bird's-eye view of Comino.

COMINO

Measuring 2.4 kilometres at its longest and 2 kilometres at its widest, tiny Comino with a mere handful of inhabitants is the 'away from it all' Maltese island. On account of its stepping-stone position between its larger neighbours it was for long a haunt of corsairs who, hidden by rocky creeks, waylaid vessels bound between Malta and Gozo. In 1618 Grand Master Wignacourt commissioned Vittorio Cassar to build the promontory fort which is a Comino landmark on the ferry crossing to and from Ċirkewwa to Mġarr. From this vantage point its guns were able to guard the island's south and west coasts and sea channels. Most of the islanders had been frightened away by the Turks, and this suited Wignacourt who turned it into another private game reserve which had become well populated with hares and partridges. Depending on class and title, poachers were severely dealt with, the punishments including heavy fines to be paid in gold, complete banishment from Malta and a period of up to three years spent as a galley slave. Similar measures were meted out to trespassers on other hunting areas in the islands.

Many visitors arrive on Comino on the boat services operated by the Comino Hotel, and it should be noted that there is no obligation to use the hotel's facilities though, invariably, tourists do. The main hotel is located at **San Niklaw Bay** on the island's fretted north coast and part of the same establishment is Hotel Nautico, a bungalow complex at the adjacent Santa Marija Bay to the east. As to be expected both are extremely well equipped, offering comfortable accommodation, good restaurants and a full range of sports and evening entertainment facilities. Their resident staff now comprises most of Comino's population, though the island still has a handful of farmers some of them working in the piggery built to restock Malta's farms following the 1980 swine-fever epidemic. In case this arouses doubt, pork is safe to eat throughout he islands.

Day visitors to Comino come for its bathing and water sports or merely out of curiosity, many of the latter spending their time walking the island's paths and tracks which are virtually free of vehicles. Ornithologists and all lovers of protected natural fauna will be gratified that this is one of Malta's bird sanctuaries where fines, if not reaching

Wignacourt proportions, are still heavily imposed on hunters. Botanists will also find much to interest them along the wild cliffs and maquis-covered inland slopes with their cover of aromatic shrubs and plants. Among them is the spice–herb cumin (*kemmuna*) once widely found on the island and from which Comino gets its name.

Composed entirely of weathered coralline limestone, the island is dry and scarred though its highest altitude is only 75 metres, in Comino Major, Comino Minor reaching 27 metres. But many of the island's edges are steeply cliffed, particularly along its north-east and south coasts. The west and north coasts are lower but peninsulared and bay-etched with deep caves and lagoona-like waters fringed by off-shore islets, **Cominotto** being the largest. It is impossible for walkers to get lost on Comino, though due care should be taken when tackling cliff-edge paths for there are many overhanging and potentially dangerous rock formations.

From San Niklaw Bay a coastal path leads westwards around **Għar Għana Bay** to **Bein il-Kmiemen**, other-wise known as the **'Blue Lagoon'**. Sheltered by Comi-notto, its exquisite turquoise-hued water is a wonderful place to swim though its paradise atmosphere is frequently disrupted in summer by the cruise boats from Malta. From here walkers can head for the **Comino Tower**, close to which is an old isolation hospital, both having served time as military prisons. Here a track offering wonderful views leads along the south coast to another redoubt, passing en route the small indentation known as **Smugglers Creek**. Skirting Comino Major to the right, a way leads north-eastwards to **St Marija Bay**, Comino's only semblance of

High cliffs and a promontory fort guard Comino's west coast

an old settlement. Here a tiny, sad looking chapel is surrounded by tamarisk trees and maquis shrubs, but mass is still weekly celebrated by a priest who comes over from Gozo. Such officialdom that exists on Comino is represented by the tiny police station at the head of St Marija Bay, another popular stopping point for the Malta cruise boats. Here refreshments can be taken in Hotel Nautico, the main Comino Hotel lying less than a kilometre to the west.

It goes without saying that Comino is no place for those in search of a hectic holiday atmosphere, yet it offers a memorable excursion for visitors staying on Malta and Gozo. Those who cling to its shores for longer, do so for reasons all their own.

APPENDIX 1 – MALTA'S GRAND MASTERS

Grand Masters of the Order of St John during its stay in Malta

Philippe Villiers de L'Isle-Adam (France)	1530–1534
Pietro del Ponte (Italy)	1534–1535
Didiers de Saint Jaille (France)	1535–1536
Juan d'Omedes (Aragon)	1536–1553
Claude de la Sengle (France)	1553–1557
Jean de la Valette (Provence)	1557–1568
Pietro del Monte San Savino (Italy)	1568–1572
Jean l'Evĝue de la Cassière (Auvergne)	1572–1581
Huges de Loubenx Vedalle (Provence)	1581–1595
Martin Garzes (Aragon)	1595–1601
Alof de Wignacourt (France)	1601–1622
Louis Mendes de Vasconcellos (Castile, Leon and Portugal)	1622–1623
Antoine de Paule (Provence)	1623–1636
Jean-Paul de Lascaris Castellar (Provence)	1636–1657
Martin de Redin (Aragon)	1657–1660
Annet de Clermont de Chattes-Gessan (Auvergne)	— 1660
Rafael Cotoner (Aragon)	1660–1663
Niccolo Cotoner (Aragon)	1663–1680
Grégorio Carafa (Italy)	1680–1690
Adrien de Wignacourt (France)	1690–1697
Ramon Perrellos y Rocaful (Aragon)	1697–1720
Marcantonio Zondadari (Italy)	1720–1722
Anton Manoel de Vilhena (Castile, Leon and Portugal)	1722–1736
Ramon Despuig (Aragon)	1736–1741
Manoel Pinto de Fonsca (Castile, Leon and Portugal)	1741–1773
Francisco Ximenes de Exada (Aragon)	1773–1775
Emanuel-Marie de Rohan-Polduc (France)	1775–1797
Ferdinand von Hompesch (Germany)	1797–1798

✖ APPENDIX 2 – BRITISH ADMINISTRATORS

Civil Commissioners

Captain Alexander Ball	1799–1801
Major-General Henry Pigot (Garrison Commander and Head of Government)	1801
Sir Charles Cameron	1801–1802
Rear-Admiral Sir Alexander Ball	1802–1809
Lieutenant-General Sir Hildebrand Oakes	1810–1813

Governors

Lieutenant-General Sir Thomas Maitland	1813–1824
General the Marquess of Hastings	1824–1826
Major-General Sir Frederic Ponsonby	1827–1836
Lieutenant-General Sir Henry Bouverie	1836–1843
Lieutenant-General Sir Patrick Stuart	1843–1847
Richard More O'Ferrall	1847–1851
Major-General Sir William Reid, FRS	1851–1858
Lieutenant-General Sir John Gaspard Le Marchant	1858–1864
Lieutenant-General Sir Henry Storks	1864–1867
General Sir Patrick Grant	1867–1872
General Sir Charles Van Straubenzee	1872–1878
General Sir Arthur Borton	1878–1884
General Sir Lintorn Simmonds	1884–1888
Lieutenant-General Sir Henry Torrens	1888–1890
Lieutenant-General Sir Henry Smyth	1890–1893
General Sir Arthur Freemantle	1893–1899
Lieutenant-General Lord Grenfell	1899–1903
General Sir Mansfield Clarke	1903–1907
Lieutenant-General Sir Henry Grant	1907–1909
General Sir Leslie Rundle	1909–1915
Field-Marshal Lord Methuen	1915–1919
Field-Marshal Viscount Plumer	1919–1924
General Sir Walter N. Congreve, VC	1924–1927
General Sir John du Cane	1927–1931
General Sir David Campbell	1931–1936
General Sir Charles Bonham Carter	1936–1940
Lieutenant-General Sir William Dobbie	1940–1942
Field-Marshal Viscount Gort, VC	1942–1944
Lieutenant-General Sir Edmond Schreiber	1944–1946
Sir Francis Douglas	1946–1949
Sir Gerald Creasy	1949–1954
Major-General Sir Robert Laycock	1954–1959
Admiral Sir Guy Grantham	1959–1962

Sir Maurice Dorman   1962–1964

Governors-General
Sir Maurice Dorman   1964–1971
Sir Anthony Mamo   1971–1974

The governors-general were representatives of the British sovereign in
Malta. Constitutionally the sovereign was recognised as head of state.

✠ APPENDIX 3 – MALTA'S MAIN BUS ROUTES

	BUS NO.		BUS NO.
Attard	40	Naxxar	54
Balzan	74	Paceville	68
Birkirkara	71.72.78	Paola	5
Birżebbuġa	11.14	Pietà	60.61.62
Buġibba	49	Qawra	49
Buskett	81	Qormi	90.91
Cirkewwa	45.48	Qrendi	35
Cospicua	1.2.3	Rabat	80
Dinġli	81	Safi	34
Floriana	*all buses*	St Andrews	68
Għain Tuffieħa	47.52	St Julians	62
Għargħur	55	St Paul's Bay	43.44
Għaxaq	8	San Anton Gardens	74
Gudja	8	San Gwann	65
Hamrun	73	Santa Lucia	15
Kalkara	4	Santa Venera	78
Kirkop	34	Senglea	3
Lija	40	Siġġiewi	89
Luqa Village	36	Sliema	62.63.64
Luqa Airport	35	Sliema (Savoy)	60
Marfa	45.48	Sliema (Ferries)	61
Marsa	5.8.11.18	Tarxien	8.11.26
Marsaskala	19	Ta' Giorni	66
Marsaxlokk	27	Ta' Xbiex	63.64
Mdina	80	Vittoriosa	1.2
Mellieħa Village	43	Wied lż-Żurrieq	38
Mellieħa Bay	44	Xgħajra	21
Mġarr	46	Yacht Marina	63.64
Mosta	53	Żabbar	18
Mqabba	35	Żebbuġ	88
Msida	60.61.62	Żejtun	26.29
Mtarfa (from Rabat)	84	Żurrieq	32.33.34

* All leaving from City Gate, but only the main routes are notated. Buses stop at intermediate destinations en route to listed termini.

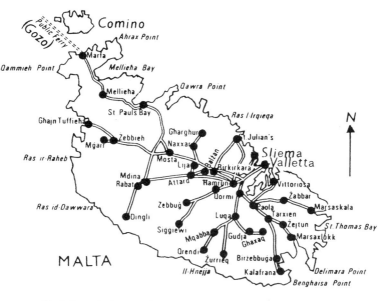

Malta's main bus routes

RECOMMENDED BOOKS ON MALTA

Eadie, P M, *Malta and Gozo (Blue Guide Series)*, A & C Black, London, 1990. A revised edition, rigorous in its historical approach and including a learned essay on Prehistoric Malta. But its clinical style and format fails to capture the atmosphere of the islands and character of the Maltese.

Blouet, B, *The Story of Malta*, Progress Press, Malta, 1981. This is a scholarly but highly readable account of the historical development of the islands and their landscape changes. It is available in bookshops throughout the islands and contains an extensive bibliography. An index would be useful for this detailed book.

Luke, Sir H, *An Account and Appreciation of Malta*, G G Harrap, 1960. A truly British account of the islands, full of personal insight and perceptive observations. Despite its date it provides entertaining pre- or post-visit reading.

Hughes, Q, *Fortress: Architectural and Military History in Malta*, Lund Humphries, London, 1969. A detailed and lavishly illustrated account of Maltese architecture and town planning.

Lockhart, D and Ashton, S, *Landscapes of Malta, Gozo and Comino*, Sunflower Books, London, 1989. A geographical guide for touring Malta by bus, car and on foot. It deals with landscape rather than history and each tour is accompanied by a detailed map.

Arbela, J S, *Malta and Gozo Explained*, Media Centre Print, Malta, 1989. An amusing account of the Maltese character and lifestyle by a well travelled native islander.

Bradford, E, *The Shield and the Sword: The Knights of Malta*, Fontana/Collins, London 1972. An in-depth account of the eventful history of the Knights of St John from the time of the Crusades to their loss of Malta to Napoleon.

Owen, C, *The Maltese Islands*, David and Charles, Newton Abbot, 1969. One of the detailed volumes in the publishers then popular 'Island Series'.

INDEX AND GAZETTEER

The number of personalities who have moulded the character of the Maltese Islands makes it impossible to mention them individually in this index-gazetteer. They are, however, mentioned in the main body of the text and include colonists and conquerors, politicians and administrators, artists and architects, poets and writers, visitors and numerous less-credentialed islanders. Appendices 1 and 2 provide chronological summaries of some important names relating to the formative periods of the Knights of St John and the British administration.

agriculture (see farming)
airlines 3, 7, 17, 85
Arabs 1, 70–71
airport 7, 10, 21, 22, 123
apartments 33
Attard A wealthy residential suburb on the western edge of the Valletta conurbation. It merges with Balzan and Lija, the townships locally known as the Three Villages, though they are now rapidly expanding residential suburbs. They all adjoin the San Anton Palace and Gardens, once the home of Grand Masters and British Governors and now functioning as Malta's official Presidential Residence. 129, 130

banks 21–2
basketball 95
beaches 91–2
bed and breakfast (see guest houses)
beers 40
bird-shooting 55–6, 120
Birkirkara One of the Valletta conurbation's main manufacturing and commercial districts. Its old quarter to the north is authentically Maltese and the parish church is regarded by many as the island's most beautiful. 128–9

Birżebbuġa Occupying one of the peninsulas of Marsaxlokk Bay, this old fishing village has greatly expanded as a tourist and trading area. The development of Freeport Malta has marred what were formerly attractive coastal views. There are small sandy beaches and a number of popular restaurants. 60, 61, 62, 88, 121–2

Blue Grotto One of Malta's main tourist attractions which in summer can be directly reached from Valletta's City Gate bus station. It is a popular stop on organised excursions. 127

Borġ in-Nadur A locality with prehistoric remains close to Wied Dalam. The temple and Bronze Age village sites are poorly preserved, but there are good examples of limestone-etched cart tracks. 60, 61, 66

British 1, 2–3, 18, 33–4, 36, 39, 45, 76–7, 86, 87 and

dgħajsa 18–19

Dingli Cliffs Named after the nearby village of Dingli (and Malta's famous architect), this is the island's coastal scenery at its most spectacular, the cliffs dropping precipitously to the sea. 48, 125, 141

diving 93–4

driving conditions 12f

economy 87–90, 116

EEC 65, 88

electricity and gas 26

embassies 20

Etna, Mount 18, 44

excursions 17–18

'fast foods' 34, 40, 96

farming 1, 5, 41, 45, 48, 50, 51, 58, 88–90, 126, 130, 134, 141, 144, 155, 158

fauna 54, 56, 140, 158

ferries 8, 16, 17

Floriana This city was built as a fortified appendage to Valletta and is encompassed by stout defences. Its street pattern is also basically gridiron, but it has more open spaces, many of them public gardens. It is named after the Italian civil engineer Paolo Floriani. 15, 32, 76, 77, 90, 98, 108–9, 114

food provisions 37–8

flora 1, 51–4, 108, 117, 129, 140, 154, 158, 160

French i, 76f, 116, 120, 121, 140

Freeport Malta 88, 122

Fungus Rock 154

geology 41f, 47–8, 134, 158

Għajn Tuffieħa A general term for Malta's rugged coast to the west of the village of Mġarr. Its popular bays and headlands are the seaward projections of the Wardija ridge. 62, 91, 142

Għammar A small village in western Gozo near to Għarb and the much visited Ta'Pinu Sanctuary. 153

Għarb A western Gozitan village with a beautiful Baroque church and authentic domestic architecture. Close by is the Ta'Pinu Sanctuary. 153

Għar Dalam A cave complex of major geological and archaeological interest in Wied Dalam near Birżebbuġa. The small museum contains a collection of primeval artefacts. 58, 61

Għar Hasan A cave complex set high in limestone cliffs with wonderful sea views. It is easily reached from Birżebbuġa. 122

Għar Lapsi One of the rugged bays along the fretted coastline south of Siġġiewi with which it has bus connections. It is popular with picnickers and walkers. 125, 127

Għaxaq Located to the east of Gudja and linked to Żejtun by the crossroads village of Bir id-Deheb. The chief attraction is the parish church of St Mary

Grand Harbour Valletta, the Three Cities and much of Malta derive their historical and current importance from this great natural waterway. *passim*

Great Fault 44, 45, (see also *Victoria Lines*)

Greeks 1, 41, 67–8, 72, 147–8

Gudja This small village is the birthplace of Geralomo Cassar and contains an interesting collection of churches. Close by is the late 18th century Dorrel Palace where both Napoleon and Nelson stayed. 123

guest houses 33–4

Ħaġar Qim A monumental temple complex reached from the village of Qrendi. Built of massive Globerigina Limestone blocks it is famous for its fat divinities on view in Malta's National Archaeological Museum. 62–3, 124, 125

Hamrun A large manufacturing and commercial town of the Valletta conurbation. Its most striking building is the church of St Cajeton. 90, 115, 128

health and medical services 25–6

hiking and walking 96, 114, 117f, 121, 125, 127, 140, 143, 144, 148, 152, 158f

hostels 34

hotels 21, 30–3

Hypogeum (Ħal Saflieni). A labyrinthine and subterranean burial complex of Temple Culture age. It ranks as one of Malta's major prehistoric sites. 60, 63–4

insects 26, 55

Kalkara Modern growth has eroded the former character of this Grand Harbour township, where the galleys of England once harboured for solace and refurbishment. Visitors might be lucky to see work undertaken on the Maltese *dgħajjes*, especially during the weeks heralding the main tourist season. 18, 116–17

karrozin 18

Knights of St John 1, 3, 45, 72–5, 78–9, 84, 85, 98f and *passim*

language 2, 69, 80, 82–3

landscape names 48, 89

lotteries 96

Luqa Known mainly for its airport, the village of Luqa was severely damaged in WW2. It contains some interesting restored churches.

'Maltafest' 97

'Malta Experience' 107

maps 14, 114

Marsa Part of the Valletta conurbation and best known for its sports centre and large industrial estate. It is also a major traffic intersection and visitors, whether by bus or car, will get to know it well. 95, 115–16, 122, 125

Marsalforn An attractive fishing village on Gozo's north coast which now reaps greater benefits from tourism. It is the main centre of holiday accommodation on the island. 16, 31, 91, 155

Marsamxett Harbour Together with the Grand Harbour, this waterway has long been responsible for the strategic value of Vallettaa and the Three Cities. Today it plays a major role in the tourism appeal of Malta, its side creeks housing large and modern marinas. *passim*

Marsaskala At the head of a long inlet on Malta's south-east coast this has become a sought after tourist venue though, to date, commercialisation has been modest. It is an ideal centre for those who enjoy coastal walks. 117

Marsaxlokk   This is one of Malta's most picturesque and visited coastal villages. It lies at the head of the eastern arm of the large Marsaxlokk Bay which has acted as an entry point since ancient times. It is a popular centre for coastal walks along the Delimara peninsula. 61, 67, 68, 88, 118, 120–1

Mdina   Malta's old capital is one of the island's major tourist attractions. This medieval hilltop city has an imposing citadel and cathedral. Crowded within its walls are palaces, churches and other early buildings. It is virtually traffic free and its modern solitude, despite the many visitors, has earned the title of 'Silent City'. The battlements offer impressive views over the Maltese countryside and the cathedral is a landmark throughout much of the island. 18, 46, 67, 70, 133–38

Mġarr   This small and attractive Maltese village is dominated by the huge ovoid-domed church, a modern structure built from local donations. There are temple ruins close by. 62, 142–3

Mġarr   (Gozo) Gozo's main port is served by regular passenger and car ferries from Sa Maison Wharf and Ċirkewwa on Malta. With its dominating churches and colourful harbour Mġarr provides a most picturesque introduction to the island. 17, 148–9

Mellieħa   This ridge-top town, the largest settlement in north-west Malta, was re-colonised in the nineteenth century. Much of it precariously clings to the escarpment of the Mellieħa Ridge which offers fine views over the broad expanse of Mellieħa Bay, a centre of modern tourism growth. 30, 33, 45, 144–5

Mnajdra   This temple complex, close to Ħaġar Qim, can be reached from Qrendi. It stands close to the sea and its stone structures are well preserved, some of them richly decorated. 62, 124, 125

Mosta   An important town close to the Victoria Lines and chiefly visited for its massive rotunda church. Mosta is a major junction for roads serving north-west Malta. 130–1, 141

motor rallies   95

Mqabba   The massive stone quarries of Mqabba are a stopping point on many organised excursions. The village itself has attractive old homes and a pleasing parish church. 123–4

Museums   Malta's museums are far too numerous to list in full. Those like the National Archaeological Museum, the National Museum of Fine Arts, the War Museum and Natural History Museum are referred to in the main body of the text, and smaller versions are found on Gozo. Many churches also have attendant museums and numerous old palaces, country houses and other interesting buildings are open to the public. The National Tourist Organisation provides a comprehensive list of what is available.

religious festivals 27–8, 84–7

religious services 26

restaurants 34f

roads 12f, 148

Romans 1, 68–9, 138f., 142, 156

Saint Paul 69, 80, 135, 143

Salina Bay This is the first major indentation into Malta's north-east coast after the Victoria Lines. Extensive saltpans developed by the Knights give the bay its name. 45, 143

San Lawrenz A small village in western Gozo with an elegant Baroque church and attractive domestic architecture. It is situated close to the spectacular Dwejra coast. 154

Sannat Gozo's traditional lace-making village close to the impressive Ta'Cenc cliffs. 32, 48, 151–2

self-catering 33

Senglea One of the Three Cities across the Grand Harbour from Valletta. It was largely destroyed during WW2 and subsequent rebuilding work can only be described as functional. It remains an important dockyard city with surviving battlements offering expansive views of Valletta.

service industries 87–8

shipping companies 8–9

Siġġiewi This agriculturally productive hilltop village is famous for its poets and its parish church, considered to be one of Malta's finest Baroque buildings. It provides a convenient centre for exploring the south-eastern section of the Rabat-Dingli Plateau. 127

Skorba Prehistoric ruins close to the village of Żebbieħ. These include early temple structures and the remains of ancient villages. It is one of Malta's earliest proven settlement sites. 58, 62, 141

Sliema This municipality has the largest population within the Valletta conurbation and it is essentially the result of 19th century and modern growth. Its older houses are much sought after by Maltese and foreign buyers with waterside views commanding the highest prices. Though lacking in beaches, this is Malta's main tourist resort. 18, 26, 30, 32, 88, 92, 96, 112–14

soccer 94–5

Spanish 1, 71, 133

sports centres 95, 116, 125, 133

St Julian's A continuation along Malta's north coast out of Sliema, St Julian's is an important resort centre. Along with adjacent Paceville and St George's Bay it is the place for restaurants, 'fast-food' establishments, late bars and discotheques. St Julian's has retained something of its attractive waterside character, but it takes the night-time lights of Paceville to invigorate what is otherwise a somewhat dreary day-time scene. 30, 32, 33, 34, 36, 92, 112–4, 143

St Paul's Bay (San Pawl il-Baħar) Now linked by coastal tourist development with Buġibba, St Paul's Bay is an old fishing village largely swamped by the influx of summer visitors.

The large bay and immediate surroundings contain many memories of the Apostle Paul. 30, 33, 45, 92, 143–4

Ta'Qali   A few kilometres south of Mosta and to the north-west of Mdina, the craft village of Ta'Qali is an important tourist venue where many authentic Maltese products and souvenirs are made and sold. 133

Tarxien   One of Malta's old and charismatic villages now linked with Paola. Its narrow, winding streets are particularly attractive, its main monuments being Damato's parish church and the Tarxien temple ruins. 59, 60, 62, 64–5, 119

taxis   8, 16–17, 27
telephones   22
television   23–4, 25, 32, 96
temperatures   (see *climate*)
theatre   96, 106
time differences   23
timesharing   28
topography   1, 43f, 48, 148, 158
trade fairs   29, 132
travel companies   30f, 35

urban growth   6, 28, 41, 43, 90, 112

Valletta   Malta's national capital occupies a peninsular site between the Grand and Marsamxett Harbours. This planned city was built by the Knights of St John in the years following the Ottoman siege of 1565. It was the fortified vision of Grand Master Jean Parisot de la Vallette and built to the grid-iron form of the Italian military architect Francesco Laparelli. Endowed with magnificent defences, great palaces, churches and other monumental buildings, it ranks as Malta's greatest tourist attraction. It is the business and financial centre of the Greater Valletta conurbation and is linked by public transport to all parts of the main island. It is easily explored on foot and contains a wealth of both visual and historical suprises. 14, 15, 18, 19, 26, 29, 30, 75, 76, 77, 78, 85, 86, 90, 96, 97, 97–108

Victoria (Rabat)   All Gozitan roads lead to this central capital which is the island's main administrative and commercial centre. The impressive citadel houses the cathedral and a number of late and restored medieval buildings, some now functioning as museums. Its ramparts offer extensive panoramas over the surrounding countryside, though the fortifications are less well-preserved than Mdina's. The centre of the town is It-Tokk and the streets that radiate from this busy market place. Wandering Victoria's streets and alleys is a photographer's delight and many crafts-people can be seen at work. 15, 16, 17, 48, 67, 85, 149–51

Victoria Lines   A series of forts and other military installations crowning the highest points along the Great Fault. These and the passes into the north-west were also fortified by the Knights to protect their main settlements and agricultural lands to the south and east. This escarpment provides some of the main island's most expansive views. 131, 132

villas   28, 33

Vittoriosa   This was the Knightly Order's first home on Malta and there are many monuments to this period including the great Grand Harbour fort of St Angelo, auberges, churches and other buildings. Many regard this city as a miniscule Valletta. 19, 68, 70, 72, 74, 110–11

water supply   24–5, 90
water sports   1, 92–4
walking   (see *hiking*)
wieds   44, 46–7, 48, 124–5, 126, 127, 132, 140, 149, 152
winds   (see *climate*)
wines and spirits   40

Xagħra   A large, irregular hilltop village close to Gozo's spectacular Ggantija temple complex. The village also has caves of prehistoric interest. 59, 62, 155–6

Xewkija   This Gozitan village is located close to the main road from Mġarr to Victoria. The massive parish church is a landmark throughout much of the island, its dimensions rivalling those of Mosta church on Malta. 149

Xlendi   An attractive fishing and holiday village in south-west Gozo. Its bay and cave-etched promontories are popular with snorklers. 16, 91, 152–3

yachting   92–3, 112

Żabbar   This attractive old casal retains much which is traditionally Maltese. Dingli's parish church is alone worthy of a visit. 116

Żebbieħ   A quiet and unassuming village in north-west Malta, visited mainly for the nearby Skorba temple ruins. Zebbieh retains an atmosphere of Maltese times past. 62, 141

Żebbuġ   Once famous for its olive groves and cotton crops, Żebbuġ is also noted for being the birthplace of a number of Maltese patriots, poets and artists. 58, 59, 126–7

Żebbuġ (Gozo)   One of the island's highest villages offering extensive views over countryside and coast. Nearby Xwieni Bay is a traditional centre of salt extraction. 154–5

Żejtun   A historical town and regional centre for south-east Malta. The parish church is regarded as one of Gafa's finest buildings. The town is an important route centre. 119–20

Żurrieq   This old casal continues to act as a main market centre. Under the Knights its surroundings supported a rich agriculture and many buildings date from this period. 124–5

Other Windrush Island Guides

MENORCA   John and Margaret Goulding

Menorca, most northerly of the Balearic Islands and the least
dedicated to tourism, has long been a favourite destination for the
discriminating holidaymaker. Its pleasant climate, pastoral countryside, gracious cities and superb beaches (many of them remote
and little visited) make it ideal for a relaxing yet interesting holiday.
Additional attractions are the island's fascinatingly varied history
and its uniquely spectacular megalithic monuments.

But Menorca also offers lively modern resorts with a high
standard of holiday accommodation. In this, the fullest guide to
the island yet published, over seventy beaches are described in
detail. In addition to chapters on history, flora and fauna, sports
and eating out, it provides a wealth of practical advice to enable the
visitor to enjoy the charm and variety of Menorca to the full.

£6.95   ISBN 0 900075 46 5   *Fully Illustrated*

LANZAROTE   John and Margaret Goulding

Lanzarote is the closest of the Canary Islands to Africa. Consequently, thousands of visitors are attracted to its modern resorts,
excellent beaches and reliable sunshine throughout the year. This
illustrated guide, the only readily available English language guide
devoted to the island, is full of practical and background
information for the holidaymaker.

The book provides advice on good restaurants, bars and
nightclubs, car hire, bus routes, taxi fares and everything from
tipping to purchasing time-share property.

There is a detailed section on touring routes and island
excursions so that the visitor can experience the unusual beauty of
the 'Island of Fire', from the fantastic geological features of the
volcanic zones to the flowery valleys of the north.

£5.95   ISBN 0 900075 06 6   *Fully Illustrated*

MADEIRA and PORTO SANTO
Andrew Gravette

Madeira has always been famous for its exotic greenery, warm climate and friendly people. Added to this list of attractions are its fine wines and unique cuisine which have made it irresistible to visitors throughout the centuries.

The neighbouring island of Porto Santo, quite different in terrain and character, with its splendid sandy beaches is also covered in this fully-illustrated guide.

This Windrush Island Guide provides advice on good hotels, restaurants, bars and nightclubs, walking tours, leisure and sports activities, the colourful festivals and Madeira's intriguing history and culture.

£6.95   ISBN 0 900075 51 1   *Fully Illustrated*

CORFU   Nigel Coleman and Conrad Mewton

Greenest and perhaps most beautiful of all the Greek Islands, Corfu has always attracted visitors lured by its stunning scenery, the rich variety of its natural history, the elegance of its capital and its wide choice of glorious beaches, many surprisingly uncrowded.

This fully-illustrated guide describes the history, culture and flora and fauna of the island, as well as providing detailed touring routes, a gazetteer and a wealth of practical information on sports facilities, eating out and nightlife – everything, in short, to enable the holidaymaker to enjoy the Corfu experience to the full.

£6.95   ISBN 0 900075 07 4   *Fully Illustrated*

Also from The Windrush Press

THE TRAVELLER'S HISTORIES

'. . . ideal "before you go" reading, putting names and places in the country's history into proper perspective'.

The Daily Telegraph

An innovative travel series which offers a complete and authoritative history of the country from the earliest times up to the present day.

Each one has a Gazetteer cross-referenced to the main text which pinpoints the historical importance of sites and towns. Illustrated with maps and line drawings, the *Traveller's Histories* are for the tourist who likes to do more than just lie on a beach.

Chronologies ● Major Events ● Famous Battles ● Kings and Queens ● Prime Ministers and Presidents ● A–Z Gazetteer ● Maps ● Line Drawings

SERIES EDITOR DENIS JUDD

ALREADY PUBLISHED

A TRAVELLER'S HISTORY OF GREECE
Timothy Boatswain and Colin Nicolson
*Paperback 198 x 129mm £7.95 320 pages Illustrated
ISBN 0 900075 55 4
Cased 204 x 132mm £11.95 ISBN 0 900075 21 X*

A TRAVELLER'S HISTORY OF ITALY
Valerio Lintner
*Paperback 198 x 129mm £7.95 288 pages Illustrated
ISBN 0 900075 60 0*

A TRAVELLER'S HISTORY OF FRANCE
Robert Cole
Paperback   198 x 129mm   £6.95   240 pages   Illustrated
ISBN 0 900075 45 7

A TRAVELLER'S HISTORY OF SPAIN
Juan Lalaguna
Paperback   198 x 129mm   £7.95   304 pages   Illustrated
ISBN 0 900075 50 3

A TRAVELLER'S HISTORY OF SCOTLAND
Andrew Fisher
Paperback   198 x 129mm   £7.95   256 pages   Illustrated
ISBN 0 900075 36 8

A TRAVELLER'S HISTORY OF RUSSIA and the USSR
Peter Neville
Paperback   198 x 129mm   £7.95   320 pages   Illustrated
ISBN 0 900075 41 4

A TRAVELLER'S HISTORY OF ENGLAND
Christopher Daniell
Paperback   198 x 129mm   £7.95   320 pages   Illustrated
ISBN 0 900075 56 2

In Preparation:

A TRAVELLER'S HISTORY OF JAPAN

A TRAVELLER'S HISTORY OF EGYPT

A TRAVELLER'S HISTORY OF THE USA

Red Velvet Cake

225g Unsalted Butter
350g Plain Flour
3 tbsp Boiling Water
1 tsp red (gel) food colour
40g Cocoa
250ml Buttermilk
1 tsp Bicarbonate of Soda
¼ tsp Salt
350g Sugar
3 eggs lightly beaten
1 tsp vanilla extract
1 tbsp white vinegar

CREAM CHEESE FROSTING

250g Butter
500g Icing Sugar
400g cream cheese
1 tsp vanilla extract

OVEN 170°c | 150° fan
300°F | Gas Mk 3

3 x 8" cake tins lined

Mix water, food colour, cocoa & buttermilk.
Sift flour, bicarb & salt in a medium bowl.
Beat butter & sugar in mixer until light & fluffy
Beat in eggs a little at a time until fully mixed then add vanilla
Turn mixer to low & add ⅓ of flour followed by ½ buttermilk
mixture. Repeat then add rest of the flour.
 Stir in the vinegar

Divide amongst the 3 tins & bake for 25-30 minutes.
Allow to cool for 10 minutes before turning out.

Sugar Cookies.

1 1/2 cup of butter
2 cups of caster sugar
4 eggs
1 tsp Vanilla extract
5 cups of plain flour.
2 tsp baking powder
1 tsp salt

Cream butter &
sugar. Beat in the eggs & Vanilla.
Stir in flour, salt & baking
powder. Chill before rolling out &
cutting shapes

Bake at 200°c

225g Self Raising Flour.
5125g butter.
125g caster sugar
1tsp ground ginger
Punch of Salt.
75g Golden Syrup
1 beaten egg

Mix all dry ingredients.
Melt butter & syrup.
Add to dry ingredients
along with the egg.
Place single teaspoonfuls
of Mix onto a greased sheet of baking
paper.

Bake for 20 minutes
160°c

Granny's Biscuits

225 g Self Raising Flour
125 g Butter
125 g Caster Sugar
1 egg
½ tsp Baking Powder
Drops of Vanilla essence & milk

Sift flour and baking powder.
Cream butter & sugar
Beat the egg and add slowly to the butter mix.
Add vanilla to taste.
Fold in the flour & enough milk to form a firm dough.
Roll out & cut into rounds.
Place on baking paper.

Bake for 10-15 min
220°c

BANANA CAKE

150 g Self Raising Flour
1/4 tsp Bicarbonate of Soda
1 ripe banana.
50g butter.
150g Caster sugar
1 egg
1/2 tsp vanilla
1/4 tsp salt.

Mix egg, banana, sugar, butter, salt
and vanilla together.
Mix to a smooth paste.
Sift in flour and bicarbonate of Soda

Bake for approximately 40 minutes
190°c

Chocolate Gateaux

150g Self Raising Flour
25g Cocoa
125g butter
1tsp instant coffee
150g Caster sugar
2 eggs
2 tbsp Milk.

Cream butter & sugar
Add eggs one at a time
Mix in sieved dry ingredients
& the milk.

Bake for 35 minutes
190°c

FRUIT LOAF

2 cups Self Raising Flour
1 cup of Water
1 cup of Dark Brown Sugar
50g butter
1 cup of Raisins
1 tsp Bicarbonate of Soda
1 egg
½ tsp mixed spice.

Put water, raisins & butter into a
 saucepan & bring to the boil.
Mix dry ingredients together & add
 the egg
Mix in the fruit
Pour into a greased 1 lb loaf tin.

Bake for 1¼ to 1½ hours
170°c

125g Butter
50g Caster sugar
175g Plain flour
1 tbsp milk

Sieve flour & add sugar
Rubs in the butter
Add milk slowly until it
forms a dough.

Roll out & cut shapes.

Bake for 15 to 20 minutes
until pale gold

180°c

Quick Chocolate Cookies

- 75g butter
- 75g sugar
- 75g light brown sugar
- 175g self raising flour
- 125g chopped chocolate
- 1 egg

Cream butter & sugar
Beat in the egg
Fold in the flour
& the chocolate.

Heap measures of 1 tbsp
onto a baking tray
leaving room for them to
spread.

Bake for 12-15 minutes

180°c

Quick Vanilla Biscuits

125g Butter
50g Caster Sugar
150g Self Raising Flour
1/2 tsp Vanilla Essence

Whisk butter & sugar
until Pale.
Add flour & vanilla and mix
until smooth.
Space tablespoons of the mix
on a baking tray
Flatten slightly with a fork.

Bake for 8 to 10 minutes
190°c

LEMON DRIZZLE CAKE

175g butter
175g caster sugar
175g self raising flour
grated zest of 1 lemon
juice of one lemon
3 large eggs
2 tbsp caster sugar

Cream butter & 175g
caster sugar
Add eggs & flour alternately
2 tbsp at a time beating
gently.
Add lemon zest.
Pour the mix into a greased
2 lb loaf tin.

Bake for 50 to 60
minutes
180°c

Add strained lemon juice to 2 tbsp
of sugar in a saucepan.
Boil for 2 minutes until the sugar
has disolved.

Remove cake from the oven & leave in
the tin.

Prick surface of the cake with a
fork/skewer & pour over the lemon
syrup.
Leave to cool in the tin

STILTON & SESAME BISCUITS

100g Butter
100g Stilton
100g Self Raising Flour
50g Sesame Seeds

Rub the butter & flour together.
Add the stilton.
Knead once or twice to
fully distribute the ingredients
Wrap & chill for 20 minutes.
Roll small pieces into 2½ cm
balls.
Roll the balls in sesame seeds.
Place the balls, well spaced, on to a
baking tray.

Bake for 10 minutes
180°C   160°c in fan oven.

CHEESE STRAWS

75g plain flour
40g butter
50g grated cheese
1/2 egg

Rub butter in to the flour
to form breadcrumbs.
Stir in the cheese
Add the egg & stir to form
a dough.

Knead lightly
& roll out.
Brush with a little egg
Cut in to strips & put on a baking tray

Bake for 8 to 10 minutes

180°c

APPLE SCONES

1 medium apple
225g Self Raising Flour
1/2 tsp Salt
1 tsp baking powder
50g Butter
50g Caster sugar
1/2 pint of Milk

Chop the apple
Rub the butter in to the flour, Salt and baking powder.
Add the sugar and apple.
Add milk until it forms a dough (soft but not sticky)

Roll out to 2 1/4" thick & 8" round.
Mark into wedges.
Brush with milk & sprinkle with demerera sugar once it is on a baking tray.

Bake for 20 to 25 minutes.
200°c

Serve warm with butter.

BACON & CHEESE MUFFINS

2 cups of Self Raising Flour
1 cup of milk
1 egg
1/4 cup of oil
1/4 tsp salt.
1/8 tsp cayenne pepper
1/4 cup of sugar
2/3 cup of strong cheese
7 strips of bacon, fried and chopped.

Mix first 7 ingredients
Fold in cheese & Bacon
Put in to Muffin tins.

Bake for 20 minutes

200°c

VICCI'S VANILLA & ROSE SPONGE

125g Butter
125g caster sugar
5ml Vanilla essence
2 eggs
125g Self raising flour
10ml milk

Cream butter & sugar
Add vanilla essence
& the eggs and whip
Sieve the flour and fold
in to the mixture.
Add the milk.
Portion in to 12 Muffin cases
in Muffin tins.

Bake for
10 minutes

200°c   Leave to cool.

4 egg whites
250g caster sugar
500g butter
1 tsp rose water.

Place egg whites in a bowl over a pan of simmering water.

Add the sugar and whisk until smooth & silky

Remove from the heat & put bowl in to the mixer stand.

Whisk until the bowl & mix are cool.

Add the butter & keep mixing.

Add the rose water.

Pipe on to cool cakes.

RICH XMAS CAKE

125g Self Raising Flour
200g plain flour.
1/4 tsp salt.
1 tsp ground mixed spice
1/2 tsp cinnamon
1/2 tsp ground nutmeg
250g butter
250g soft dark brown or dark Muscovado sugar
2 tsp black treacle.
5 eggs
50ml of alcohol or cold tea
1 1/2 tsp vanilla extract
900g raisins
250g chopped dates
50g ground almonds or swap for plain flour.
Finely grated rind of 1 lemon
3 - 4 tbsp brandy.

Grease and line a 9" round or 8"
square tin using double thickness
grease proof paper.
Wrap a double thickness of brown paper
round the outside of the tin standing
5cm above the top of the tin.

Sift flour, the salt, mixed spice, cinnamon
& nutmeg in to a bowl.
In another bowl cream the butter & sugar
until light.
  Add the treacle beating.

Lightly beat the eggs alcohol/tea and
vanilla extract.
  Gradually beat in half of the egg mixture
in to the creamed butter mix. Fold in
1/3 of the flour.
  Continue to add the eggs & flour alternately

Mix in all the remaining ingredients
except the brandy.
Turn in to the prepared tin and smooth the
top.

  Bake for 3 to 3½ hours until a
skewer comes out clean.
      140°c

Leave to cool in the tin.
Prick all over and pour over the brandy
store in an airtight tin to mature for
approximately 1 month before icing.

FONDANT ICING

Also called SUGAR PASTE & ROLLED
FONDANT.
Used to cover a cake. A fruit cake
should be marzipaned first. A sponge
doesn't need marzipan but two layers of
FONDANT is recommended instead

ROYAL ICING

Made from Icing sugar, water and
merri-white (powdered egg white).
Used for piped decoration & run outs.
Kept in an airtight container it will
last for a week or two.
When decorating a cake either keep the
spare icing in its container with its lid
on or cover the container with a damp
cloth. This will prevent the icing forming
a crust.
Royal Icing can also be frozen.

PETAL PASTE

Also called FLOWER or GUM PASTE. This
can be used in moulds & to make
flowers & models. Models and flowers

work best when the petal paste is mixed with FONDANT. This increases the time it takes to dry giving you more time to create the flower/model.

ROYAL ICING RECIPE

½ oz Merri-white   500g Icing sugar.
         water.

½ oz merri-white = 1 rounded dessert spoon
       OR   10 ml.

Dissolve the merri-white in 3 fl oz (80 ml = 8 dessert spoons) of water. Leave for a few minutes to fully dissolve.
Put half the sugar in a mixing bowl.
Add the egg white & mix on slow.
Once the sugar & egg white are combined add the rest of the sugar and mix until fully incorporated.
Turn up the mixer speed & mix until it forms fairly stiff peaks

FLOWER/PETAL PASTE

2 lbs Icing Sugar
6 tsp Gum Tragacanth
4 tsp/2 strips of Gelatine
10 tsp cold water or 9 water & 1 vanilla
    essence to disguise the taste of the gum
4 tsp Trex/White Flora (Vegetable shortening)
4 tsp Liquid Glucose.
2 egg whites - use merri-white mix

Dissolve the gelatine -
        If using the powder place the water in
        a cup & put the gelatine on top &
        leave for at least one hour.

        If using the strips put in a bowl or
        cup of water for 5 minutes. Remove &
        squeeze dry. Add the .10 tsp of water
        to the rest of the mix.

In a microwave/heatproof bowl add the
Trex, Glucose, Gelatine & water.
    Then either —
        Place bowl over a pan of boiling water
        & mix until everything has dissolved

OR   Microwave for 2 x 1 minutes.

In your food mixer bowl add the sugar
gum tragacanth & egg white.

Once cool add the gelatine/Trex mixture
& stir gently with a dough hook.

When all of the sugar is incorporated
turn the speed up & knead in the mixer
for about 5 minutes.

Remove from the mixer & put in a food
bag. Double bag into a freezer bag &
put into the freezer.

Once frozen the paste can be cut
in to more manageable portions &
re-frozen until needed.

Makes 100g,

MAKE A PIPING BAG

Use good quality parchment paper

Create a triangle of paper

8"-10"
Approx

Hold the point on the right.
Bring the top point down &
round to meet the middle point
on the side facing you.

middle point. top point meets it

Bottom point is then curved over
the top to meet the back of the centre
point.

This now forms a cone

Turn the cone so the 3 points
are together at the top of
the cone opening. and
furthest away from your body.
Hold the points between your thumbs &
index fingers inside the cone (thumbs) &
fingers at the back of the points.
Move the inside & outside points to

create a small sharp point at the bottom of the cone. This is best done by moving the points upwards rather than left & right

Fold the three points together in to the cone creating a circular opening.

The bag can be used with or without nozzles to decorate.

Run Outs

Split a quantity of Royal Icing in to two pots. Thin one pot down to the consistency of double cream.
Put this into a piping bag without a nozzle.
Put the thicker mix into a bag with the nozzle you want to use.
Using the nozzled bag (a No 2 is good) create the outline. Tape a piece of paper with the picture on to a cake board/flat surface. Tape parchment paper over the top & pipe the outline.
Pipe one section at a time then flood the section with the looser mix icing.
Continue in this manner until all sections are done.
Allow to dry fully in open air, for approximately 5 days.

Good Madeira cake recipe —
LINDY SMITH's from "CELEBRATE WITH A CAKE"
will last 7 - 10 days in an air tight
container

Fruit Cake —
MAISIE FANTASIE's "PARTY CAKES"

CAKE COVERINGS

ROUND	FONDANT	MARZIPAN
6"	750g	600g
8"	1 kg	800g
9"	1·5 kg	1 kg
10"	1·75kg	1·25 kg
12"	2·25 kg	1·75 kg
14"	3 kg	2·25 kg
16"	3·5 kg	2·85 kg

SQUARE		
6"	1 kg	750g
8"	1·5 kg	1 kg
10"	2 kg	1·5 kg
9"	1·75 kg	1·25 kg
12"	2·5 kg	2 kg
14"	3·5 kg	2·65 kg
16"	4 kg	3 kg